POPULISTS AND PROGRESSIVES

The New Forces in American Politics

POPULISTS AND PROGRESSIVES

The New Forces in American Politics

Steven Rosefielde
University of North Carolina, Chapel Hill, USA

Daniel Quinn Mills
Harvard Business School, USA

World Scientific

NEW JERSEY · LONDON · SINGAPORE · BEIJING · SHANGHAI · HONG KONG · TAIPEI · CHENNAI · TOKYO

Published by

World Scientific Publishing Co. Pte. Ltd.
5 Toh Tuck Link, Singapore 596224
USA office: 27 Warren Street, Suite 401-402, Hackensack, NJ 07601
UK office: 57 Shelton Street, Covent Garden, London WC2H 9HE

Library of Congress Cataloging-in-Publication Data
Names: Rosefielde, Steven, author. | Mills, Daniel Quinn, author.
Title: Populists and progressives : the new forces in American politics /
    Steven Rosefielde, Daniel Quinn Mills.
Description: Hackensack, New Jersey : World Scientific, [2020]
Identifiers: LCCN 2020004249 | ISBN 9789811217180 (hardcover) |
    ISBN 9789811218408 (paperback) | ISBN 9789811217197 (ebook) |
    ISBN 9789811217203 (ebook other)
Subjects: LCSH: Political culture--United States. | Populism--United States. | Progressivism
    (United States politics) | Right and left (Political science)--United States. | Presidents--United
    States--Election--2020. | United States--Politics and government--2017–
Classification: LCC JK1726 .R738 2020 | DDC 306.20973--dc23
LC record available at https://lccn.loc.gov/2020004249

British Library Cataloguing-in-Publication Data
A catalogue record for this book is available from the British Library.

For any available supplementary material, please visit
https://www.worldscientific.com/worldscibooks/10.1142/11744#t=suppl

Desk Editor: Dong Lixi

Typeset by Stallion Press
Email: enquiries@stallionpress.com

CONTENTS

ABOUT THE AUTHORS

Steven Rosefielde, Professor of Economics, University of North Carolina, Chapel Hill. He received his PhD from Harvard University and is a Member of Russian Academy of Natural Sciences (RAEN). His books include: *Democracy and Its Elected Enemies: The West's Paralysis, Crisis and Decline*, Cambridge University Press, 2013; *Inclusive Economic Theory* (with Ralph W Pfouts), World Scientific, 2014; *Global Economic Turmoil and the Public Good* (with Quinn Mills), World Scientific, 2015; *Transformation and Crisis in Central and Eastern Europe: Challenges and Prospects* (with Bruno Dallago), Routledge, 2016; *The Kremlin Strikes Back: Russia and the West After Crimea's Annexation*, Cambridge University Press, 2016; *The Trump Phenomenon and Future of US Foreign Policy* (with Quinn Mills), World Scientific, 2016; *Trump's Populist America*, World Scientific, 2017; *China's Market Communism: Challenges, Dilemmas, Solutions* (with Jonathan Leightner), Routledge, 2017; *The Unwinding of the Globalist Dream: EU, Russia and China* (with Masaaki Kuboniwa, Kumiko Haba and Satoshi Mizobata, eds.), World Scientific, 2017; *Putin's Russia: Economic, Political and Military Foundations*, World Scientific, 2020.

Daniel Quinn Mills provides thought leadership in several fields including leadership, strategy, economics and geopolitics. He has been a director of publicly-listed firms and is currently a director of several closely-held private corporations. He has published books about business activities, the media, American foreign policy, economic policy, and political processes.

During the Vietnam War, Mills spent several years in Washington, DC helping to control inflation. For several years, he was in charge of all wages, prices and profits in the construction industry (then fourteen percent of GDP). Simultaneously he taught at MIT's Sloan School of Management. Thereafter he taught at the Harvard Business School. He has done consulting and speaking in the following countries: United States, Canada, the United Kingdom, Indonesia, Ireland, France, the Netherlands, Germany, Switzerland, Italy, Russia, Israel, China, Japan, Malaysia, Brazil, Columbia, Mexico, Singapore, South Africa, Kuwait, the United Arab Emirates, Saudi Arabia, Vietnam and Australia.

Mills earned his MA and PhD from Harvard, both in economics. He received his undergraduate degree from Ohio Wesleyan.

Throughout his career, Mills has been an influential author. His most recent books are *Authoritarians Resurgent: Rethinking Global Security* (with Steven Rosefielde), forthcoming 2020; *The Trump Phenomenon and the Future of US Foreign Policy* (with Steven Rosefielde), 2016; *Global Economic Turmoil and the Public Good* (with Steven Rosefielde), 2015; *Shadows of the Civil War*, 2014; *The Leader's Guide to Past and Future*, 2013; *Democracy and Its Elected Enemies* (with Steven Rosefielde), 2013; *The Financial Crisis of 2008–10*, 2010; and *Rising Nations* (with Steven Rosefielde), 2009. Previously he published *Masters of Illusion: Presidential Leadership, Strategic Independence and America's Public Culture* (with Steven Rosefielde), 2007.

PART I

NEW FORCES IN AMERICAN POLITICS

The politics of a modern democracy are replete with paradoxes, ironies, and contradictions. One of the greatest paradoxes of modern American politics is that while the populists hold the presidency, they do not hold a major political party (conservatives control the Republican Party; and while the progressives do not hold the presidency, they are almost within control of the Democratic Party and may gain it this election cycle). Without a populist political party to back his presidency, President Trump cannot move a populist agenda forward in Washington in any significant way. The progressive movement, however, may be able to advance its agenda and someday gain the presidency if it captures the Democratic Party.

Therefore, progressivism is much more important in American political life now than populism. We will therefore devote more pages to progressivism than to populism in our first chapters.

CHAPTER ONE

A TIME OF CONFUSION

Americans are used to our political battles being between conservatives and liberals. But, in the past few years, new forces have jumped to the forefront. Conservatives are now being displaced by populists; liberals by progressives. Populists do not care much about conservatives — they cooperate with them but without enthusiasm. Progressives dislike liberals — they are trying to eliminate them.

The presidential election of 2016 was fought between populists and liberals and was won by populists. The presidential election of 2020 will be fought between populists and progressives and will be won by …? That question will be answered in depth by this book.

The emergence of populists and progressives as major factors gives a new face to politics in America — one that is full of significance for the future.

How this happened and what it means is the subject of this book.

Our objective is to clarify the muddled rhetoric and reporting about current politics. Politics is changing dramatically and neither the media nor the politicians themselves have kept up. Media reports are garbled, like talking about love with the language of friendship. The terms are just off — they do not convey the reality, but that is all the media has. So confusion is rampart.

Even the best commentators write or speak with only two categories for American political competition — two categories which each have two labels. Conservatives are Republicans. Democrats are liberals. There was once a strong logic to this. Conservatism is the ideology of Republicans — to the extent that they have one. Liberalism is the ideology of Democrats, and most Democrats have an ideology.

However, we have now added populists and progressives to the lexicon. Almost all commentators simply treat *populist* as a synonym for conservative (or reactionary), and *progressive* as a synonym for liberal. This is profoundly wrong. Populists are not conservatives, and progressives are not liberals. In fact, populists are as different from conservatives as they are from liberals; and progressives are as different from liberals as they are from conservatives.

As much as progressives and populists differ from each other, they have more in common than they have with liberals or conservatives. Progressives and populists have their roots in the same reality of American politics today — the rejection by large segments of the electorate estranged from the establishment comprised mostly of Republican conservatives and Democrat liberals. The situation is fluid and perplexing.

To try to describe the American political spectrum today, we need to employ a number of terms. We move from the far left which is characterized by the facemasks and violence of *anti-fa* (anti-fascist) to the far right characterized by the prejudice and violence of the neo-Nazis. Though they differ in ideology, anti-fa and neo-Nazi are similar in tactics and in hatred of their opponents.

We move from the anti-fa to the progressives on the left and from the neo-Nazis to the populists on the right. From the progressives on the left to the liberals and from the populists to the conservatives on their left. Liberals are the core of the Democratic Party; progressives lie to their left. Conservatives are the core of the Republican Party; populists lie to their right.

With these distinctions clarified, we can now discuss the American political spectrum with accuracy. It is a rule of politics that one's most bitter rivals, even enemies, are always in one's own party. This is because people in one's own party are far more apt to have stifled a person's own ambitions than are people on the other side of the spectrum. Thus, it should be no surprise that progressives and liberals are bitter opponents, and that populists and conservatives disesteem each other.

To avoid writing about something they neither understand nor have the vocabulary to describe accurately, most American commentators retreat into diatribes about political personalities. Because he is in the White House, Donald Trump is the greatest victim of this phenomenon. However, the political issue in America today is much bigger than Trump, though he plays a role in it.

Trump was elected on a populist platform by a populist upsurge, and as president, he has tried to satisfy his populist majority, with mixed results. The establishment in Congress, both Democrats and Republicans, and in the courts, have thwarted him. Now as a candidate for re-election he again makes promises to the populist majority, but the political dynamic has moved beyond where it was four years ago. The tension today is between populists and progressives, with the progressives much on the climb. They attack Trump unceasingly. They would do so to any opponent. This reality is missed by the many observers who believe that the 2020 election is primarily about Donald Trump. It is not. It is a contest between populists and progressives, in which many American voters, probably a deciding electoral margin, could decide to go either way — to vote populist or progressive — not because they are independents of the old style — uncertain between Republicans and Democrats — but because populists and progressives vie with each other to attract the allegiance of the disaffected segments of the American electorate.

Nonetheless, it is hard to discuss American populism without discussing Trump, despite the fact that populism is a much broader movement. This is because populism is ill-organized and ambiguously defined. Trump has been elected as its champion and so it is necessary to turn to him for clues as to its deeper nature. The risk however is that American populism is identified with the personality and political fortunes of a single man, Donald Trump, and this may do it great damage.

One of the characteristic responses to Trump's presidency has been to seize upon an analogue and narrate Trump's presidency in that way.

One analogue has been European fascism. Another is Latin American populism.

American populism is thereby characterized as either European fascism (ethnic exclusionary nationalists) or Latin American populism (have-nots against the haves), or, by some magic, a combination of both. When media and commentary narratives about American populism are crafted, pundits look not to American populism itself, but to European fascism or Latin American populism as the basis for the narrative. This is fabrication — a fictional thing. It misrepresents reality. For example, the difference between American populism and Latin American populism is distinct and significant. Latin American populism stresses big government as a tool for serving have-nots. It is socialist. American populism stresses small government and is anti-socialist. They are thus antithetical not similar. Nonetheless, the term *populism* is applied to both. The use of the term *populist* cannot be controlled, but it is important to point out that American populism should not be equated with and tarred by Latin American socialism.

Opponents characterize American populism with diametrically opposite labels. For example, progressives paint populism as fascist reactionaries. Conservative free traders — who oppose American populism's willingness to employ tariffs — paint populists as isolationists. So which is American populism — is it socialism, fascism, isolationism? Or, perhaps it is contrarianism or reactionaryism?

It is none of the above. Populists are America's yeomen and commoners, once viewed as the "salt of the earth" in the Frank Capra movie of the 1930s, *Mr Deeds Goes to Town,* or idealized in Grant Wood's painting, *American Gothic,* who have become today's surrogate for Ralph Ellison's "invisible men." The Democratic and Republican Parties both claim the common people as their constituents and pretend to service their needs through big government spending but treat a large segment of them as untouchables. Populists do not want the Democratic and Republican Parties' big government, and are further aggrieved knowing that they are being overtaxed and under-served for the benefit of other groups and special interests (Wall Street and social activists). Populists are treated as stepchildren and know it. The Democratic and

Republican Parties know it too but do everything in their power to divert attention from the issue by portraying populists as riffraff. They expect to succeed because, just as the proletariat of yore, the benighted *rabble*, as the establishment perceives populists, do not have big monied support. They are *small pocket* outsiders who can be steamrolled.

There is no correspondence whatsoever between the establishment's caricature and contemporary American populist reality. Populism in the United States today is an unorganized, spontaneous movement seeking the downsizing of federal power vertically in order to restore an open society, democratic free enterprise, equal opportunity (not affirmative action, entitlement, and restorative justice), traditional values, patriotism, optimal immigration, and protection against predatory foreign competition (especially from China).

The media disregards all these attributes. It portrays populists as enemies and progressives as champions of the open society, when the truth is just the reverse. This is why it is so important to describe American populism as it actually is.

A similar confusion applies to American progressivism. It is described by many as analogous to European socialism and the accompanying narratives are crafted by critics of European socialism. The analogy is misleading. The essence of European socialism has been anti-capitalist, anti-free enterprise, pro-blue-collar working class, and pro-industrial nationalization. American progressives advocate these policies only in the special case of healthcare. While American progressives continually attack big business, they seem to have made political accommodation with it — preferring to regulate rather than nationalize it. Much of American big business supports American progressivism.

There is, of course, an American socialist movement which is much closer to European socialism than American progressivism. Senator Bernie Sanders, an advocate of *entitlement socialism* has given well-publicized voice to this movement in recent years as he has run for the Democrat nomination for president. American socialism today is big government "entitlement socialism for the masses," not the far more radical Marxist revolutionary socialism. There is substantial support in America for the practice of "entitlement socialism," but mostly under the guise of the welfare state championed by both the Democratic and Republican parties. Support for entitlement socialism and revolutionary socialism formally led by political parties remains small. Four socialist parties participated in the 2016 presidential election. They collectively received 91,890 votes out of the 138 million votes cast. Although socialist voices are increasingly loud, socialism is not the centerpiece of either American liberalism or progressivism.

Critics of progressivism describe it as a form of entitlement or revolutionary socialism, trying to tar progressivism with a socialist brush. Similarities are asserted to be identities. However, American progressivism is neither European entitlement socialism (sometimes called democratic socialism or Fabian socialism), nor revolutionary Marxist–Leninist–Stalinist socialism. It is important to describe progressivism in its own terms, not with some fancied analogy.

We try to describe American populism and American progressivism as they actually are — by their elements displayed in the United States. We do not present portraits of either based on false analogies.

The increasing tension between progressive and populist in American political life will continue whether or not Mr. Trump remains in the nation's political spotlight.

This book is about that change and what it means for the future. There is no single, clear truth, but there are different perspectives which claim validity. We offer different perspectives including how populists and progressives see themselves, how they present themselves to the public, and how each sees the other.

CHAPTER TWO

REVOLT OF THE MIDDLE CLASS: THE POPULIST RIGHT

Populism in America is a revolt of the silent majority; the common people in the middle and working class against the establishment that increasingly treated them as political outsiders and riffraff. The blue-collar working class and the common people were the darlings of the left during the Roosevelt years, but were gradually shunted aside after the 1950s. Populism has its roots in widespread resentment at perceived inequities in society touching the silent majority, the working and other segments of the middle class. They are overtaxed, their moral and religious values are under assault by progressives, and their real and relative incomes are eroding due largely to the action and inaction of the federal government, Republicans, Democrats, and the establishment.

The federal government today no longer even bothers to protect unemployment insurance which has been significantly cut by shortening the duration of the benefit period. It prefers instead to divert spending from the unemployed to progressive projects. Populists seek an overthrow of an entrenched regime intent only on serving others. In a democracy, it seeks its victories at the ballot box.

Populism is ordinarily met — as it has been in the United States, the United Kingdom, and the European Union in recent years — by strong resistance from the establishment and the establishment's political allies, committed to overtaxing and under-serving the silent majority, the middle and working classes. The rich avoid paying and the poor cannot pay. The middle foots the bill.

Populism won significant political victories in its emergence only a few years ago, in the United States with Trump's election to the presidency, and in the United Kingdom with the success of the Brexit referendum. Both Trump's election in the United States and Brexit's victory in the United Kingdom have been met with unrelenting opposition from the establishment and other political opponents. Both have only a tenuous hold on power.

What is populism in America? Like all political movements, it is a complex mixture of many elements. It is easier to describe it than to define it.

In recent times in America, populism has viewed itself as a political revolution aimed at overturning the establishment's economic policies and the left's progressive social agenda both at home and abroad. Populism's assault on the establishment can be interpreted as reactionary anti-establishment iconoclasm, but it is more than that. There is a sort of grand design. Populism seeks to roll back America's progressive social justice agenda to 1960 when equal opportunity and self-reliance took precedence over affirmative action and restorative justice. It wants to roll back America's worker protection policy to the 1930s when preserving industrial jobs and shoring up wages took precedence over free immigration, and family was more important than cosmopolitanism. It wants to roll back federal government regulation to the 1920s, eradicating stifling executive orders, mandates, controls, and management, and fostering economic prosperity. It wants to roll back America's international commercial policy to 1913 when trade and finance operated on a level playing field and America was not subject to self-serving, beggar-America policies of other nations like China. It wants to restore a fundamentalist interpretation of the Constitution to our courts and small government to Washington. It wants to make America the world leader based on its pre-World War II ideals and economic prowess. In all this, populism is profoundly tradition-driven and backward-looking for its ideal policies. It seeks to turn the actual past to the service of the future. Hence the popularity of President Trump's slogan — *Make America Great Again.*

At first glance, the populist agenda may seem contradictory. Trade liberalization, barriers to international migration of labor, and tariff walls appear incompatible. However, this is not necessarily so. Populism seeks limited liberalization consistent with restrained immigration and symmetric regulation of trade. For example, it objects to China protecting its markets while demanding free entry for its goods into the United States.

Although populism's desire to advance America's global leadership position based on the traditional values of an open society and bilateral treaty ties rather than chic elitist progressive values and global alliances may seem antique, the approach could be better than the European Union's crumbling transnationalism.

Populists propose that an America based on an open society, anti-left ideals, and sundry pragmatic compromises could be the basis for a durable American prosperity and international leadership.

Populists want dramatic change with an orientation toward the economic and social status of the majority of a nation's current population and reinforcement of national traditions. They are strongly patriotic, supporting both the nation's military and its police and quasi-police (like the Border Patrol and Immigration and Customs Enforcement) forces. Strongly nationalistic, they are suspicious of the motivations and actions of foreign nations. In today's United States, they feel that our erstwhile foreign allies have unfairly benefitted from our largess and wish to reverse that situation.

The Attitudes of Populists

Washington's expenditure processes appall populists. Agencies talk in terms of absorptive capacity (how much money can the agency take and spend) and being part of the pipeline (the flow of federal funding to the agencies). Agencies spend much of their effort pushing money out the door so that all the appropriation they have received is spent and they can ask for as much or more money for the next budget cycle. Populists are troubled by people who go to Washington to curb waste, fraud, and abuse but find themselves frustrated by the system. Populists (and conservatives) see the behavior of agencies as waste, fraud and abuse, and wish to have the tax dollars that fund it returned to taxpayers. This is a very different attitude from that of elitist progressives who prefer government spending to private spending and seek generally to increase government spending come what may.

Populists are meritocratic. They want to be rewarded for their effort, not penalized for it. They support Stalin's disdain for "parasites," that is, people who exploit other people's honest labor.

Populists are pro-productive. They want their hard work to be effective and the foundation stone of national prosperity. They disdain supercilious free riders (many progressives).

Populists seek more rapid economic growth. They recall the high growth rates of the 1960s and early 1970s, not approached since. They believe the United States economy has the potential to grow much more rapidly. When they won the presidency, they proposed a group of reforms that would provide more rapid growth. Their purpose was to provide more and better jobs to industrial workers (not government civil servants), to provide for reduction of the federal debt, and to provide resources for strengthening America's global presence, including our military. A series of policy actions let to an economic growth rate of some four percent early in Trump's presidency — a rate of growth more than double that which Trump had inherited. However, it did not last. The establishment was uncomfortable with so fast a rate of growth. Conservatives generally seek a lower rate of growth in order to permit large firms to maximize profits. A slower rate of growth gives employees less opportunity to reduce profits by seeking pay increases. It also permits large firms to maximize profits by better resisting new competitors — for whom rapid economic growth provides opportunities to get a foothold in markets — and by maintaining the most profitable rate of growth, which is a moderate rate. The Federal Reserve (Fed) is ordinarily sympathetic to the conservative point of view and soon raised interest rates, slowing the economy. The complaints of the populists were futile, and the President was widely criticized in the media for attempting to interfere with the independence of the Fed. The tax reform legislation proposed by the President and enacted in a very different form by the

Republican-led Congress failed to generate the hoped-for rate of business investment. By the end of Trump's third year in office, the American economy had settled into a roughly two percent annual rate of growth and the President, seeking to make the best of a disappointing result, was joining conservatives in proclaiming that the American economy was racing ahead at its two percent rate of growth.

The Democrats did not participate in the political struggle over the rate of growth except to criticize the President for criticizing the Fed. In general, led by progressive views, the Democrats are no longer concerned with the rate of economic growth and industrial workers. They focus instead on affirmative action civil service jobs for minorities and the redistribution of income and wealth.

Rapid economic growth is a top priority of populists. Conservatives place a high priority on slow to moderate rates of economic growth. Progressives focus on increasing entitlements and taxes, the purpose of which is redistribution, and would gladly tolerate negative economic growth if it furthered the causes of entitlement, affirmative action, and restorative justice.

Populists as yeomen and common people tend to feel themselves to be members of the majority, so they should be able to exercise authority, but are frustrated by the want of strong leaders to do it.

Populists remind us that the dictionary definition of populism is merely power to ordinary people.

CHAPTER THREE

POPULISTS ARE NOT CONSERVATIVES

Populism and conservatism are very different political philosophies. The media has taken notice. For example, labeling populism as "the new right," the *Economist* attacks it by contrasting it with conservatism:

> The new right is not an evolution of conservatism but a repudiation of it…. Consider how they are smashing one conservative tradition after another. Conservatism is pragmatic, but the new right is zealous, ideological and cavalier with the truth…. Conservatives are cautious about change, but the new right now airily contemplates revolution…. Conservatives are suspicious of charisma and personality cults…." ("The Global Crisis in Conservatism," *Economist*, July 6, 2019, p. 9.)

The *Economist's* characterizations flatter conservatism and libel populism. Populism is far more pragmatic today than conservatism. Populism has no ideology, even though it has a vision of a good open society free from abusive special interests. Conservatism, by contrast, has formulated over the past several decades a rigorous and rigid ideological position that has driven it into a small corner of the national political arena.

Populists and conservatives now share occupancy of the Republican Party rather like feuding neighbors who occupy a house for two families. Conservatives are very jealous of the electoral success of the populists in gaining the presidency and feel that the crown should have been theirs to wear. They view themselves as the legitimate successors of Ronald Reagan, and they view Reagan's Administration as the exemplar of what American government should be. Populists, on the other hand, have no special reverence for the memory of Reagan, viewing him as the president who set in motion the shift of American manufacturing jobs to the Far East, first to Japan and later to China. He was also the sponsor of what became the North American Free Trade Agreement (NAFTA) which led to the transfer of millions of more American jobs out of the country. While conservatives revere Reagan's memory, populists do not.

Despite these differences there is, of course, an overlap between populists and conservatives because both populists and conservatives want economic growth as the preferred way to advance national prosperity, placing environmental concerns, including opposition to climate change, at lower importance. Populists seek jobs and conservatives seek business expansion that may lead to more jobs.

In the high priority that both populists and conservatives place on traditional forms of economic growth, they encounter strong resistance from other elements of the American political spectrum. The left places an increasingly high priority on environmental concerns. Because of environmental concerns, there is a strong constituency in the United States for slow economic growth. Nonetheless, there are other members of the slow-growth group as well. Large companies maximize profits at slow rates of growth. Many well-to-do Americans prefer slow growth because it is less disruptive to their communities and lifestyles. The Federal Reserve System prefers slow growth because it ensures looser labor markets and this helps keep inflation low. There are many who have adjusted to and profit from a slow growth economy. These groups constitute a strong constituency for slow economic growth. They have created a slow-growth mindset widespread in America.

Populists have struggled against it for years. President Trump has sought to have US economic policy drive a higher economic growth rate. Part of this effort was to lessen Chinese advantages in trade with the United States. Opposition to this is strong, though usually denied. For example, Charlie Gasparino, a commentator on the Fox Business

Network, in the late summer of 2019 called on Trump to fire Peter Navarro, his Director of Trade and Industrial Policy. Gasparino said Navarro might cost Trump the election in 2020. Then came an acid test of Trump's populism: would he fire Peter Navarro who was arguably the only true populist (committed to trying to improve the lot of the working people of America) in his economic coterie, or would he stand by him and keep to the promises he made to get elected? If he fired Navarro, he would have signaled that he had joined the conservatives of the Republican Party and would run with them for re-election. Trump did not fire Navarro. He maintained his trade policy stance vis-à-vis China, signaling his continued commitment to his populist base of support.

A populist policy agenda is different from a conservative agenda, just as it is different from an agenda drawn from the left — from progressives or liberals. For example, a populist agenda stresses economic growth intended to provide good jobs to industrial workers. It favors tax reform which treats working people as well as it treats the rich; it does not favor tax concessions to corporations and the wealthy — which is sometimes a high conservative priority; it does not favor repeal of the Affordable Care Act — in contrast, this is a high conservative priority.

The *Economist* is not the only commentator to urge a negative interpretation of populism. To liberals and progressives, and even to many conservatives, *populist* and *demagogue* are synonyms. Populists reject this accusation. Instead, they assert that the demagogues are in the establishment, and their target is the populists.

For example, the former head of the World Bank, Robert Zoellick, has turned his attention from domestic issues to American foreign policy and criticizes populism.

> Mr. Trump's foreign policy reflects his instinct for political realignment at home, based on celebrity populism. Populist movements feed off grievances and impatience with traditional politics. Frustrations — whether generated by economic distress, social displacement, or cultural challenges — fuel skepticism about institutions and elites. Challengers (who want to become the new elite) attack traditional leaders as out of touch, incompetent and corrupt.

Mr. Trump rallies his supporters by proclaiming the three presumptions of populism. First, it professes to reflect the will of a scorned people. Hillary Clinton called them "deplorables." The will of the people is intolerant of Washington's excesses, and disdains the identity politics of the Democratic Party.

Second, populism finds and blames enemies, domestic or foreign, who thwart the people's will. Mr. Trump has mastered insulting such scapegoats.

Third, populism needs "the leader," who can identify with and embody the will of the common people. Like other populist leaders, Mr. Trump attacks the allegedly illegitimate institutions that come between him and the people. His solutions, like those of other populists, are simple. He contends that the establishment uses complexity to obfuscate and cover up misdeeds and mistakes. He claims he will use his deal-making know-how to get results without asking the public to bear costs.

Mr. Trump's foreign policies serve his political purposes, not the nation's interests.... His style of deal-making prizes uncertainty and brinkmanship, without a plan for what comes next.

(Robert B. Zoellick, *The Peril of Trump's Populist Foreign Policy* quoted in *The Wall Street Journal*, November 29, 2017.)

To populists, this is a grossly unfair and self-justifying establishment mis-characterization.

PART II

WHEN LIFE ISN'T GOING RIGHT, YOU SHOULD GO LEFT: THE PROGRESSIVE MOVEMENT

Progressivism is the most energetic political movement in America today. Senator Bernie Sanders is right when he says that it has changed the American political conversation since the presidential election of 2016.

CHAPTER FOUR

PROGRESSIVES ARE NOT LIBERALS

During the third debate between the Democrat presidential candidates that took place mid-September 2019, an exchange of the following nature occurred.

Former Vice President Joe Biden related some of his efforts to help disadvantaged people improve their position in life. He mentioned that children in disadvantaged homes had a much smaller vocabulary when entering schools than did children from more advantaged homes. Limited vocabulary was a factor in holding back their academic performance. In order to help improve the children's vocabularies, their parents were urged to turn on the radio in the home so that their children would hear a wider vocabulary.

Senator Biden was immediately ridiculed for his statement. Many of Biden's opponents on the debate stage were honestly perplexed. Many of the media commentators openly questioned why Biden had referred to the radio during his response to a question about the disadvantaged. They insinuated that Biden was losing his clarity of thought due to age. They fitted his comments into a growing narrative that Biden was too old and too addled to be President.

However, what was really happening was a conflict between the liberal and the progressive mode of thought. Biden is a liberal. He was simply expressing the self-help aspect of liberal approach to poverty — which is to provide parents and children in disadvantaged families with affirmative action skills to get ahead in the competition for education and jobs, that is, to equip them to compete better in our society. The example Biden used was the coaching tip of employing the radio to expose children in poor families to more words than they would ordinarily learn from their parents, and so better equip them for success in school.

Biden's critics, of his own political party, had no idea what he was referring to since their concept of poverty, its causes and what to do about it was the opposite of his. They were progressives, not liberals.

To the progressives, to suggest, as Biden did, that the disadvantaged were poor because of their own limitations (in this case of vocabulary) instead of being permanently scarred victims of historical injustice was outrageous. It was so politically incorrect that they could not recognize the notion when spoken even by a Democrat candidate for president. To progressives, the poor are poor because they were and are exploited and discriminated against by the American social and economic system, not because they fail to help themselves. The proper policy to deal with society's victims is to compensate them (social entitlements and reparations); to munificently provide them with special opportunities (affirmative action); and to radically change the nation's social and economic system in their favor. It is certainly not to coach them on how to improve their vocabularies. Michael Harriot's *woke* attack on Pete Buttigieg provides another vivid example of the enmity progressives feel toward liberals. (John McWhorter, "The Woke Attack on Pete Buttigieg," *Atlantic*, November 27, 2019.)

Similarly, Michelle Obama — who is a sophisticated political person — appears to be a liberal rather than a progressive, at least at this time. On March 21, 2014, Michelle Obama defended her efforts to combat child obesity in this way: "It's not about how the children look; it's about how they feel."

She said this to avoid criticism of her efforts by progressives. She feared that progressives would criticize her for being more concerned about culturally disapproved physical traits than how obese people feel. According to progressives, people should not feel ashamed of their appearance, even in the case of extreme obesity. They should flout traditional cultural norms. So Michelle Obama could act only in order to improve the feelings — the emotions — of children. She could not recommend improving their appearance or their health, though she was very concerned, appropriately, with her own appearance and health. Liberals want to help the disadvantaged conform to traditional norms; progressives want to replace traditional norms with their own politically correct standards.

The conflict between the liberal *hand up* and the progressive *unlimited entitlement and reparations* approach is fundamental to illiberal leftist politics in America. When the Democrats are out of power, the conflict between traditional and radical values is ignored by liberals and progressives as they join hands to try to defeat Republicans. However, when the left attains power, whether in Congress or in the presidency or both, the conflict comes to the forefront. This is because liberals stress the social need for equal opportunity, basic entitlement, and minority diversity in our institutions, while progressives stress the immediate gratification of the aspirations of those they consider society's victims deserving of restorative justice. Liberals want victims to become self-sufficient; progressives want them indemnified.

Affirmative action is a policy which can fulfill both social and moral objectives, but the two objectives often conflict when restorative justice is a priority. For example, the need for social diversification can be met by immigration of minorities from abroad. The need for restorative justice cannot.

Liberals worry that restorative justice in the form of monetary reparations to African-Americans will leave African-Americans in exactly the same place in American society a short period of time after the reparations have been paid. In their view, affirmative actions to improve the skills of minorities are crucial to a long-term solution to the problem. Progressives favor an unending sequence of financial reparations coupled with the direct quota allocation of positions and jobs to minorities with little or no regard to competency. They are impatient, viewing liberalism as an excuse for doing nothing. "Justice delayed is justice denied," in their opinion. This is the underlying conflict which Biden's remark revealed in the third Democratic debate.

In this brief confrontation, the wide difference in thought and attitude between liberals and progressives was clearly on display. So also was what to many people is the defining character of progressivism — its definition of *political correctness*. Political correctness (the latest version of what Marxists used to call the Soviet communist *party line*), is a body of tabooed speech and expressions that is not tolerated by progressives. It is an effort to pre-emptively control political debate by stigmatizing opponents' language and concepts. Notice that correctness in the term *politically correct* does not imply that a policy is good, moral, or true. It only means that it is politically expedient, like the Molotov-Ribbentrop Pact signed in Moscow September 23, 1939.

So strong has political correctness become and so widely recognized in America that many liberals, conservatives, and populists are acutely aware of its strictures, and they either do not violate the unpublished rules of political correctness or, when they do violate political correctness rules, they themselves call attention to it. "This is not politically correct," a person will say, "but I'm going to say it anyway." In his comment about radios in the third debate among the Democrat presidential hopefuls, Joe Biden had grievously violated the taboo of political correctness and was not even aware of it.

What is politically correct changes frequently. For example, a few years ago, we could refer to *American Indians*. Then that became politically incorrect and was followed by the term *native Americans*. The two terms referred to the same group, but were said to reflect different attitudes toward them. Then *native Americans* was superseded by *indigenous people*, implying their rights as victims of white colonialism to entitlements, affirmative action, and restorative justice. This currently is the approved term. In a later chapter when we make reference, we will use *indigenous people*, hoping not to offend progressives.

Why these frequent changes? In part, they reflect a continuing revision of history by progressive scholars to justify the progressive agenda. In part, they are a way to identify the more loyal of progressives — that is, those people who keep up with the twists and turns of approved language among progressives.

The story above about Joe Biden and the third debate was about how progressives differ from liberals in thinking about society and the government response to economic and social shortcomings. That

Biden later recognized and was able to state clearly the difference between liberals like himself and progressives in the fall of 2019. Speaking on behalf of liberals, Biden described progressive spokesperson Senator Elizabeth Warren as an elitist who was not in touch with the people. He added that the progressives were saying to the people, "If you were as smart as I am, you'd see that I'm right about everything."

Progressives also differ from liberals in how they take action for political purposes.

A conservative acquaintance (he was definitely not a populist) told me:

> I can give you a perfect example of the difference between progressives and liberals. One summer's day I was at my vacation home and about 20 people arrived outside. They pulled out signs and began shouting in my front yard. They were very abusive and, when my wife and children looked out of the house, the demonstrators called them names for being in my family. The police came and kept the level of noise and action down. My neighbors were straining to look outside their houses. The whole neighborhood was disrupted. At one point, I tried to go outside to talk to them, but the abuse soared to a new level of noise and I had to slip back into my house. It was an unpleasant hour; one that frightened my family. Later that day I walked down into the village where our house sits. I went into store after store and was told: "I saw the people who came to your house. I am a Democrat, too, and I do not agree with your politics. However, I respect you and your opinion. I am not one of them and I don't support what they did to you this morning."

The demonstrators were progressives. The local people were liberals. The demonstrators were radical and sanctimonious. The local people were tolerant. That's the difference.

There was intimidation in this incident, but no violence, but violence is always feared at conservative and populist gatherings. Anti-fa are a self-named, self-organized, action-oriented arm of the progressive movement. In recent years in the United States, they often appear in the streets wearing black stocking caps with eye holes so that they cannot be identified. Generally, they are young people and seem to be most prevalent around college campuses. They confront conservative or populist supporters, sometimes violently. They may be viewed as the militant wing of progressivism. They are one of the very few armed and violent wings of an American political party. They may be the only one that has existed on a large scale.

The modern background of the anti-fa are the student demonstrators (mobs) which terrorized college campuses and sometimes poured onto the streets to oppose the Vietnam War. Sometimes police controlled them; sometimes they were ordered by town officials not to — as with anti-fa today. When the protests by violent gangs ranged too far from college campuses and began to draw national media attention, a reaction developed.

At that time, I (Mills) was teaching two days a week at MIT and working three days a week in Washington to help stabilize the economy. Part of my government work allowed me to have continuing contact with the building trades including contractors and labor unions. Thus, I was in an unusual position to watch one of the major political episodes of the time.

Universities provided demonstrators against the war. They grew increasing aggressive in the streets and in their actions. Deciding that he must respond to them, President Nixon rejected calling on police (most big cities were run by Democrat mayors who refused to control the demonstrators) and the military (it was unpopular because of the Vietnam War). Instead, he urged construction workers (so-called *hard hats*) to meet the demonstrators in the streets and match them violence for violence. Hard hats poured out of construction sites with the approval of their unions and employers. There was no contest. Prime age, tough workers, carrying tools as weapons, many veterans among them — they dispersed the college students quickly.

The students returned to their campuses where the President asked the hard hats not to follow — and they did not.

This is not a promising solution for dealing with today's anti-fa. Student activists are available for the anti-fa, but hard hats have dwindled in numbers and political activity and may not be available at the call of a Republican President. Anti-fa may have a longer and more successful run than did the Vietnam War demonstrators.

Progressives do not hesitate to condemn liberals as being hardly better than the hated leader of American populism, Donald Trump himself. Taking Joe Biden as a symbol of liberalism, progressives attack him directly.

> What if Joe Biden wins? It could mean long-term trouble for Democrats. Sure, the former veep is "better than Trump." However, his presidency could sabotage the Democratic Party's future. Everything fundamental that made Trump possible in the first place is going to continue, unless something sweeping and extraordinary is done to counter it — and that's precisely what Biden's "return to normalcy" argument assures us will not be done.
>
> A would-be President Biden will not get much more cooperation from the GOP than Obama did, but he will continue to play nice, babbling on about his "good Republican friends" only to have them tar him with everything that goes wrong as a result. All this will make massive midterm losses in 2022 even more likely (à la 1994 and 2010) and will position the GOP to run a more professional and disciplined Trumpist to defeat him in 2024. (Paul Rosenberg, https://www.salon.com/2019/08/31/what-if-joe-biden-wins-it-could-mean-long-term-trouble-for-democrats/, August 31, 2019.)

Progressives are different from liberals in how they think and behave, of which we have given examples above. For Liberals, Thanksgiving is a day to celebrate national harmony, mistreatment of native Americans notwithstanding. For progressives, it is a day of infamy with no redeeming aspects. Progressives despise liberals, including liberal leadership in the Democratic Party.

In addition, to understand today's Democratic Party, a person has to understand progressivism as much or more than traditional liberalism, because progressives are coming to dominate the Party. What do progressives say they favor? Is that also different from liberalism in whole or in part?

Progressives want dramatic — not gradual — radical change in America. They want their order, not the existing one. They want to overthrow what they claim is a *white-male-dominated oppressive social, political, and economic order* and replace it with a fully entitled and recompensed *progressive rainbow coalition* (excluding white males and other riffraff). They demand radical — not limited — change. They want revolution — not evolution. They are not satisfied with progress, despite their name — *progressives* — they want a full transformation of our economy and society. They are sanctimonious about their revolutionary ambitions. They are Mensheviks in spirit now, but have the mentality to become Bolsheviks tomorrow.

To attain these goals, progressives propose a massive extension of the welfare state and restrictions on speech and ownership of guns. They are internationalists and favor unrestricted immigration. They have major ambitions abroad but oppose pursuing those ambitions with military force (until they come to power). For example, they promote human rights and regime change in many countries abroad, but denounce efforts to achieve those goals, and others besides, by use of American military force.

We will see later that opponents of progressivism denounce what is said to be its increasing advocacy for *entitlement socialist* schemes (as distinct from Marxist–Leninist–Stalinist revolutionary programs). Rising world entitlement socialist sentiment for have-nots (that sometimes includes the working class) is consistent with progressive interpretations of universal ideals like the rights of man (but not white men, conservatives, populist riffraff, and, perhaps, liberals), rationality, fraternity (for the politically correct), liberty and equality (for progressives only). If humans are fundamentally alike, have the same rights and view one another with respect, then it is reasonable for those advocating entitlement socialism in one country to shed their nationalism and strive to construct a politically correct inclusive global socialist order that shares and protects every progressive have-not without regard to geography, gender, race, ethnicity, or religion. Entitlement socialism in one country from this perspective is narrow-minded at best, and no more than a waystation on the road to world socialism (for progressive *adorables*).

There is no reason to expect entitlement socialist sentiment, both of the progressive and liberal strains, to subside in the United States and elsewhere. Demands for open immigration that foster racial, ethnic, and religious diversity are mounting, while resistance to world entitlement socialism among liberals is diminishing. The entitlement socialist (and progressive) tide has been rising for at least a half century. Thus, the Democratic Party's two wings — liberal and progressive — are moving closer together in support of different varieties of modern entitlement socialism (not Soviet-type communism). Modern entitlement socialism is not focused on government ownership of the means of production (with the exception today in the United States of medical care) as was Marxist–Leninist–Stalinist revolutionary socialism, but instead is focused on increased entitlement programs paid for by partially confiscatory taxes on populists (working lower and middle classes) and the wealthy.

In addition, progressive-sponsored campaigns to compensate the descendants of former European and American colonies and slaves for past abuses are intensifying. The appeal of radical feminism is increasing everywhere. Calls for egalitarianism, stakeholder sovereignty, and transnationalism, and against liberalism and neo-liberalism are waxing across the globe. If these trends persist, the character of political regimes in both East and West will become more entitlement socialist of the progressive or Fabian type, verging toward revolutionary socialism.

Progressives tend to be people who feel on the outside and identify with some sort of minority — ethnic, gays, or even women, who are not a minority at all, but for whom radical feminists are a leading-edge minority.

Progressives are far more ambitious than liberals. They aspire to dominant all aspects of life, including education, and make many false claims about their innovativeness. For example, Elizabeth Warren is a leading progressive and was for decades a university instructor. We are now told that her teaching method is radically progressive.

What is Warren's innovative progressive teaching method? It is calling on students in her classroom to answer questions without informing them in advance that they will be getting a call. This is so-called *cold calling.* It is a technique that has been used at the Harvard Business School for more than 100 years and has never been conceived of as politically progressive. Yet now a progressive writer informs us that "Warren's version of the Socratic method, cold-calling on students in her law courses, is actually deeply progressive." We are also informed that academic progressivism is now thoroughly radical — not just taxing the rich, but rejecting an entire way of life. (David Gooblar, "What Elizabeth Warren Can Teach Us About Teaching," *Chronicle of Higher Education*, September 4, 2019.)

What is the way of life that is being rejected? It is a way of life that admires and rewards performance. It is a way of life that centers on merit. As described in the *Chronicle of Higher Education*:

> [There] seems to be the emerging bipartisan consensus. "On the evidence we have, the meritocratic ideal ends up being just as undemocratic as the old emphasis on inheritance and tradition," writes *New York Times* columnist Ross Douthat. "Our supposedly meritocratic system is nothing but a long con," declares Alanna Schubach, a college-admissions coach, in Jacobin. "Merit itself has become a counterfeit virtue, a false idol," argues Daniel Markovits, a professor of law at Yale University, in a new book, *The Meritocracy Trap* (Penguin Press, 2019)." And meritocracy — formerly benevolent and just — has become what it was invented to combat. A mechanism for the concentration and dynastic transmission of wealth and privilege across generations. ("Afternoon Update: Is Meritocracy Hurting Higher Education? A Chronicle Forum," *Chronicle of Higher Education,* September 13, 2019.)

The rejection of merit represents a complete repudiation of the traditional society, just as progressives say. It is akin to nothing so much in history as the French Revolution with its total rejection of monarchy, aristocracy, and religion (but not progressive reason and pseudo-science); and nothing else so much as the Russian Revolution with its complete rejection of nobility, bourgeois virtues and religion. It is hard to see how American progressivism could become any more radical without openly embracing a Bolshevik-style revolutionary *coup d'etat.*

This is a deep part of progressivism, reminiscent of the *Wobblies* [Industrial Workers of the World (IWW)] and is completely new to the post-war American political discussion. The policy implications seem to be something like this, though progressive spokespersons have yet to articulate them to the national audience — female, minority, and challenged students who score F are good; A students are bad, and they should accept the authority of F students.

CHAPTER FIVE

THE END IS ALL-IMPORTANT

A key feature of elitist-led progressivism, like Bolshevism, is that it places the end above all means — progressive entitlement above fairness to others — and affords itself almost unlimited means to attain its objectives. That is, the end justifies all means. *Playing hardball* is the most basic of political presumptions — that there are no rules but power. The purpose of power is said to be to advance the good causes of the political movement, but it becomes an end in itself as it did under Marxist–Leninist–Stalinist communism because power can be used to pursue any objective, including hidden or newly developed ones.

There is a playbook developed in 1930s by the Nazis and the Communists (Reds) in their conflict with one another. Though they were bitter enemies and professed very different ideologies, they were in important respects very similar. Neither had any scruples about the methods used to defeat the other. Politically correct obligation to their causes trumped everything else. Over time, both used the same methods. Among the most popular was to accuse the other side of doing what the accusing side was already doing or going to do. That allowed the Nazi or communist side making the accusations to claim that when it was discovered doing the thing, the discovery was only another false political claim by its adversary. Further, since Nazis and communists were using the same unscrupulous playbook, any general accusation made about either side was likely to be true.

For example, many of today's claims made by the progressives are not true. But the progressives have from the beginning accused extreme right leaders of the populist movement of lying to the American public. In the instance of Donald Trump, progressive media (in particular the *Washington Post*) published repeatedly a count of lies which Trump had supposedly told the public. Soon the list of Trump's lies was in the thousands. The inventory however was also inflated. For example, whenever Trump denied the accusation that he had collaborated with the Russians during his 2016 Presidential campaign, his denial was counted as a new lie. [The accusation was refuted by the Mueller Report (see an excellent review of the findings of the Mueller Report published in that most establishment of journals, *Foreign Affairs*, by Stephen Kotkin) (Stephen Kotkin, "American Hustle: What Mueller Found — and Didn't Find — About Trump and Russia," *Foreign Affairs*, July/August 2019.)]

Thus, Trump was accused of something he didn't do, and when he denied it, that was counted as a lie he had told. When denial of lies is counted as a lie, then the total of so-called lies can add up quickly.

This is not an exoneration. Trump doubtlessly sometimes lies. However, this is not extraordinary. Lies are common in politics and in diplomacy. Asked once why he had lost the Democrat nomination in 1992 to Bill Clinton, one of his opponents, a distinguished Senator and veteran of the Vietnam War, replied, "You have to remember that he is just a better liar than any of the rest of us."

A friend, a Washington attorney, once said to me, "You don't really think Mrs. Clinton lies to us, do you?" I had to shake my head in surprise. "Yes, of course, she does," I (Mills) replied, "and so does her opponent."

It would be common at this point to deplore that untruth is common in politics. But that would be to pretend a naivety that no adult in a democracy should possess. Human beings are imperfect, and no more so than in their dealings with each other in politics. Nonetheless, there are degrees, and progressives are suspected by others of having no more scruples about the tactics they use in political conflict than did the Nazis and the Reds.

The Crucial Role of Radical Feminists

Feminists are a somewhat loosely defined movement composed of women with strong political and social objectives based on equally strongly felt grievances. The movement has many male sympathizers. It is an artefact of social change and the Age of Reason, especially the French Revolution, and has been gaining momentum for nearly 250 years.

Not all women are radical feminists, certainly not a majority, and some women strongly oppose radical feminist attitudes and activities. Nonetheless, a large proportion of women who are not radical actively support much of what radical feminists demand and do. This is similar to the attitude most Muslims have about the radical fringe of Islam whom we Westerners generally label terrorists. A majority of Muslims support many things that radicals want, although they may disown their methods. This means that radical feminist leaders have a much more significant role in our politics than their numbers suggest. And almost all radical feminists are progressives.

Radical feminists maintain that their purpose is to rectify an eternity of discrimination (perhaps 4 million years) by men against women that continues to this day. Feminists propose to accomplish this revolution not by liberal equal opportunity, but through privileges and restorative justice. Radical feminists reject criticism as ill-concealed efforts to maintain male privileges and perpetuate discrimination against women.

Critics insist that radical feminists want the privileges that they claim men monopolize. They want to behave like men and hold their jobs. Movies today show women beating up men in single combat and pursuing men sexually as men have pursued women in the past; feminists want into the military and into combat, and they reject all *bourgeois* distinctions — *lady* is a stereotypical differentiation that perpetuates discrimination against women; it is not, as its users may think, a compliment. Radical feminists reject all the traditional feminine virtues and aspire to all the traditionally male attributes. At the heart of progressivism is political radical feminism. Liberals until recently thought that they had a political monopoly on feminism at the polls. Now, progressives decry the liberal stress on women's equality as archaic.

Moral Superiority

During the decade before our Civil War, in the middle of the 19th century, Congress passed, and the President signed, a Fugitive Slave Law. It permitted slave owners to pursue runaway slaves into any part of the United States. Law enforcement officers were to assist them in catching fugitive slaves. From its inception, abolitionists denounced the Fugitive Slave Law and refused to be bound by it. They continued to help slaves escape bondage. They concluded that the law does not always have progressive morality on its side. They learned that the law can be flouted, and that, eventually, a law they considered immoral could be changed. The law, they had learned, is not sacrosanct. There are immoral laws that people who believe themselves righteous can and should disobey.

Slavery ended, but racist *Jim Crow* laws continued to exist in much of the country. The Civil Rights movement of the mid-1900s featured disobedience to those laws. Ultimately, the laws were changed.

Progressive and liberal opposition to today's immigration laws has its roots in the tradition in American politics of opposition to laws considered unrighteous. Thus, it is that populists and conservatives insist on compliance with American law, and progressives and many liberals insist of flouting current immigration laws.

Progressives and many liberals view illegal immigrants to the United States as the modern counterpart of fugitive slaves — struggling against an immoral and unfeeling governmental authority. They characterize the government's enforcement actions of immigration laws in exactly that way. They are indignant at the perceived immorality of the government's actions and are sympathetic to the suffering imposed on immigrants and their families.

This viewpoint, when contrasted with an alternative viewpoint of support for duly adopted laws of the nation, creates what is at this point a seemingly irreconcilable political dispute. The issue is not about the details of immigration law, but about broad attitudes toward government and morality.

Preferences for Favored Demographic Groups

In the *Chronicle of Higher Education* of May 22, 2017, Kelly Field wrote, "Most community college leaders are white men. The next generation demands diversity." (Kelly Field, "What Will It Take to Change the College Presidency?" *Chronicle of Higher Education*, May 22, 2017.) It is notable about this statement that the article made no claim that the white men who are currently leading community colleges are doing a poor job, or are incompetent, or corrupt, or any of many other possible failings, but instead in Bolshevik style demanded their ouster simply because they are white men. Liberals favor the advancement of women and minorities who are as good or better than the white males they replace. Progressives make no such qualifications. To a progressive, any woman or member of a minority group is favored over any white man. She is entitled and deserves preferential quotas to achieve restorative justice. Here again progressives abandon all thought of merit in the award of positions and compensation and rely entirely on gender or race for preference. Their illiberality does not embarrass them. They are proud of being avenging angels.

Deep Philosophical Roots

Our discussion of populism and progressivism may make each sound more internally consistent than it is. Both are riddled with inconsistencies. Populism makes no effort to achieve policy or ideological consistency. It has no ideology and advances what it believes are the values of America's pre-Vietnam War past. It wants an America for the common people without worrying much how the elements fit together. In this respect, it is very unlike conservatism, which has think tanks, scholarly journals, book publishing houses, and theoreticians. Conservativism serves wealthy segments of the business community. It seeks full ideological consistency and prides itself on the effort.

Progressivism has an ideocratic agenda (various ideal policy goals) selectively borrowed from Marxist politics rather than an integrated and comprehensive ideological worldview. It has a party line that is continually changing, but it expects full compliance with every twist and turn. It enforces adherence via its effort at political correctness. For example, it is a key tenet of progressivism that European and American internationalism is simply colonialism — that is, racism and exploitation. Yet, currently, progressive thinkers are urging an alliance between a progressive-led United States and the European Union as a key element of American foreign policy.

Progressives, focused on their domestic objectives, are currently borrowing foreign policy prescriptions from the liberal establishment without reconciling the contradictions. For example, the Center for American Progress has published a proposal entitled *A New Progressive Approach for Reviving the Trans-Atlantic Alliance*. The new progressive approach starts with the observation that:

> The E.U. has the geopolitical potential of a rising power.... A new administration should seek to forge common approaches with the E.U. on a broad swath of critical issues, including climate change, economic prosperity, foreign policy, and arms control.
>
> America and the E.U., working in tandem, can drive the global agenda and ensure that the 21st century moves in a liberal and democratic direction. The U.S. should pivot toward Europe and once again fully support and encourage its continued integration and partner with it internationally. (Max Bergmann, *Embrace the Union: A New Progressive Approach for Reviving the Trans-Atlantic Alliance*, Center for American Progress, October 31, 2019.)

That is, progressivism now urges the United States to join with European internationalism that it bitterly condemns as colonial exploitation and warmongering.

Concerned with the inconsistencies in progressivism's patchwork ideocracy, a few progressive intellectuals are trying to create a coherent ideology. For example, Joseph Stiglitz has published a book entitled *People, Power, and Profits: Progressive Capitalism for an Age of Discontent* (W.W. Norton, 2019). The book seems intended to create a comprehensive economic ideology for progressivism. The creation of an ideology will empower progressivism by transforming progressivism from a motley collection of ideocratic causes, many of which are rivals, into a movement. The ideology Stiglitz's offering draws so heavily on socialism that it seems to its critics almost the same set of arguments with a different label — progressivism.

Despite lacking a cohesive ideology, the philosophical roots of progressivism are deep. As they appear in our time, they are these.

1. **Technological determinism.** All is new. What was impossible yesterday inevitably will be possible tomorrow. For this reason, nothing from the pre-progressive past matters, other than past atrocities that justify contemporary radical action. All that matters is rectifying past injustices in the present, and we can see the world changing even more in the future due to technology — a form of technology determination. It is the progressives' version of Fritz Lang's film, *Metropolis* (1927).
2. **Humanism.** Progressives are good souls. They are true humanity. When all the peoples of the world become progressive, humanism will reign universally.
3. **Taste has nothing to learn from the past.** Taste is what progressive leadership likes and radical chic taste is dictated by progressives' current political position. In the big cities, progressives consider themselves trendsetters and dismiss the tastes of everyone else as *passé*.
4. **Anyone with contrary ideas is riffraff.**
5. **The ends justify all means.** In pursuing our convictions, the ends justify the means.

It seems to their critics that progressives, like their Marxist–Leninist–Stalinist predecessors, do not sweat the details. They have some key high-minded notions and goals, but they change rapidly. They are untroubled by their inconsistencies — what critics view as double-talk.

CHAPTER SIX

HISTORY AS THE SERVANT OF PRESENT-DAY POLITICS

Napoleon said, "It is my knowledge of the past that reveals the future to me." What he meant is that history reveals patterns of human behavior which are reflected in the present and future. Rejecting all knowledge of the past except that which is chosen for its usefulness in current political controversy, insisting that history has no other value, progressives seem to have no framework for imaging the future, so they make it up out of their own desires, and it is wholly an illusion. They live in a romanticized fantasy-world, both domestically and in foreign relations. From this expedient free inventing emerge *dreams* that become their policies.

Rejecting all knowledge of the past, insisting it has no relevance, progressives have no bead on the future, so they make it up out of their own desires and it's wholly a delusion. They live in a hallucinatory — world, both domestically and in foreign relations.

As I (Mills) once heard a progressive history teacher explain, "There is a common misconception that a history course is the study of the past." If it isn't the study of the past, what is history? It is the study of the present with some of its progressive antecedents thrown in. That is, it is a study of racism with some of racism's foundations described. It is a study of discrimination against women with some of the bad behavior of men in the past illuminated. History is immediately relevant politically.

The progressive view of American history is a long story of slavery, discrimination, exploitation, injustice, inequality, and violence, with little else. The land was stolen by violence from its rightful owners — indigenous peoples. Slaves were imported to build wealth for whites. When slavery ended, racial discrimination became rampart. Working people were exploited by capitalists. Women were systematically abused by white men. The judiciary supported the oppressors. Systematic mistreatment continues and only the political victory of progressivism can end it.

The cherry-picked past casts a long shadow over our present. We are captives of fictive pasts in many ways — both in terms of what happens and in terms of how we interpret it. As William Faulkner is said to have commented, "The past isn't dead, it isn't even past." Instead, the caricature of the past is fully alive today and influencing us. We cannot escape its influence; not even by trying to revise it. Progressives assiduously revise history to manipulate contemporary thinking.

For progressives, history has a role in current politics. Any attempt to recreate a balanced picture of what really happened in the past is politically incorrect. And since the needs of current politics change rapidly, history has to be revised continually. Progressives, like Stalinists before them, freely re-invent history to fit their current political positions. In our universities today, history is often taught in a very selective and often fictive fashion to fit progressive political postures. For example, as evidence that Europeans came to the Americas in the 16th century and destroyed highly civilized nations of indigenous people, the story of the Spanish conquest of Mexico is told. But certain key matters are omitted. That the Aztecs were history's largest-scale practitioners of human sacrifice is expunged from the narrative, despite the skulls of thousands of Aztec victims being discovered only recently in the center of Mexico City. Also, the defeat of the Aztecs in the siege of Mexico City is attributed entirely to a few hundred Spanish conquerors, while the fact that the Spaniards were joined in the siege by more than 100,000 indigenous American non-Aztecs is omitted. History is edited Soviet- and Nazi-style to make it fit a progressive position that Europeans have always persecuted indigenous peoples. Furthermore, modern American progressivism is part of a long line of socialist positions put forward in the United States and other countries at least since the French Revolution. Many have failed — as in the Soviet Union. Each time one variety fails, supporters move on to another.

If they kept track of their failures, and the 100 million plus killed in progressive experiments (see Steven Rosefielde, *Red Holocaust,* Routledge, 2010), it would be difficult to continue their pursuit of progressive goals. Progressives, however, prefer tunnel vision. They focus exclusively on bad aspects of the current system, without reflecting on the bad historical consequences of their *foolproof* methods. For the most part, they find it convenient to forget about the bad consequences of their past methods and cannot contemplate the possibility of their repetition. Biased history and selective amnesia therefore are employed to conceal the truth.

Progressives have no difficulty justifying their biased rendering of the past. They are proud of it. The end justifies the means. When confronted with the accusation, "You're making the past up," they will respond, "Yes, we are; we are pointing to the better future that we envision. We are creating the future with our technology and our aspirations." It is our duty to make lies come true.

The Rich Should Pay

Progressives abhor income inequality. Senator Bernie Sanders believes there should be no very rich people. He considers it a moral outrage that there are billionaires. Senator Elizabeth Warren proposes a tax on high wealth. Senator Sanders proposes to tax high incomes at over 90 percent (which was established practice during the 1930s under Franklin Roosevelt). Medicare for all will require higher taxes on the middle class — Senator Warren denies this, but knows better. Senator Sanders admits it, but finds solace in the misleading claim that the savings of middle-class people on health insurance and health costs will outweigh the additional tax for the same quality of medical service.

Government Entitlements Outweigh Individual Choice

Progressives believe in munificent government entitlements for their followers. They disdain everyone else, and do not want to let non-progressives passively resist by opting out of government programs. Liberals are very different. They prefer government options, combined with flexible choice. Liberals are willing to let people make choices about healthcare and other matters in which government takes a role. Liberals proposed, and still support, a government option for health-care — that is, a government-provided healthcare program like Medicare that any American could choose to join. Progressives oppose this. They demand a compulsory general coverage government healthcare program that puts an end to private insurance.

Progressives recognize that the financial viability of many government-provided entitlements require that all people participate — so giving people a choice about participating is likely to undermine the programs. Also, progressives prefer progressive big government action over individual choice as a matter of moral choice and/or ideology.

Progressives do not share the liberal and conservative notion that there is value to individual choice (except for themselves and their constituencies). Like Marxist–Leninist–Stalinists, they perceive a history of individual choice that eventuates in race and gender discrimination, inadequate government programs, and environmental degradation, and see no moral or political advantage to individual choice. Progressive government choice, they contend, is always preferable to individual choice.

Sources of Progressivism

As we have noted, many of the most celebrated current leaders of progressivism are radical young women. This gives the movement its *au courant* flavor.

Progressivism has a foundation in the far left's past. Many of Obama's and Hillary Clinton's advisors were Marxists. At first, they were Soviet apologists, or European-style advocates of social democracy.

Then when the Soviet Union collapsed and China went to a form of market economy, these people kept awaiting a re-emergence of Soviet-style communism.

Finally, they gave up and moved to a new political home. They provide support to the younger generation of progressives who are now emerging. For the most part, these people consider themselves democratic socialists aligned with Bernie Sanders.

We should note that there are different degrees of progressive commitment to entitlement, affirmative active, and restorative justice programs, some of which, like Elizabeth Warren's (universal healthcare) or Alexandria Ocasio-Cortez's (Green New Deal) are more radical than Sanders' entitlement socialism. The progressive agenda is vastly more expensive than Sanders' socialist projects. If the progressives prevail, then their programs for their followers will crowd out some socialist entitlements for the many.

Media and Schools: The Core Strength of Progressives in the United States

Critics of the left have complained vigorously about the preponderance of leftist views on college campuses. Two examples will illustrate the complaint. Writing in the *Chronicle of Higher Education,* a professor tells us that, in the past, he had always told his students that they had the right to think differently about political issues than he — in fact he had encouraged them to do so. However, he discovered that tolerance has become outdated. It is no longer good enough. He recently wrote:

> With the election of Donald Trump, my approach has now changed. Some things are not up for debate. I am not that comfortable with it, but I feel that I have no choice. Trump does not simply confront us with different political opinions; he challenges and erodes basic American values. There are far too many to list; but here are a well-known few: his undermining of a free press by excluding critics from access to the White House, the prejudice he exhibits when he tells immigrants to go back to where they came from, his open admiration of dictators like Vladimir Putin, his equating of hate speech with rightful dissent,

his personal denigration of political rivals with petty nicknames, and the vile way he speaks about women. (Joseph P. Viteritti, "How Trump Changed the Way I Teach," *Chronicle of Higher Education*, September 22, 2019.)

Another writer tells us:

We first must dispense with the myth of the politically neutral classroom. All educational spaces are political. Even if instructors do not disclose their ideological stances, their beliefs can be found in the structure of their syllabi, the readings they assign, the students they call on during class discussions, and the non-verbal expressions they — often unknowingly — make. Intent here is immaterial; by merely engaging in the act of teaching, one is sending political messages to students. (Wayne Journell, "Professors, Are You Hiding Your Politics? Bad Idea," *Chronicle of Higher Education*, September 22, 2019.)

Of course, the politics that will be revealed most of the time are progressive.

Progressivism insists that speech is frequently action, blurring the distinction between the two. Traditionally speech is action only when it is like yelling "Fire!" in a crowded theater and causing a stampede of people which injures some. For progressives, any language which might offend someone — for example, using the term *master*, which might offend African-Americans because it recalls slavery, is an action that requires atonement. Because of this blurring of speech and action, freedom of speech is constricted. Universities in particular have been limiting speech and are frequently in court facing accusations that they are violating the Constitution's First Amendment which guarantees free speech to Americans except in highly unusual circumstances.

American schools are full of such professorial conceits, and ordinarily they are not up for discussion. The first professor quoted above focused on the personality of Donald Trump — probably as he divined it from the mass media. Other faculty members devote attention to public issues, not only political personalities, and generally with a leftish orientation. Organizations have grown up among conservatives to try to offset the left-lean of the universities, of which the most prominent today is Turning Point USA.

The core strength of the progressive left in American politics is its dominance of media and the universities. That is, control of information and education. The media conveys control of the present — news is spun to the left's advantage. Education conveys control of the future — the young people have been indoctrinated. The progressive agenda is championed on the air and in the schools. If the left's control of information and education continues, the right will be marginalized toward oblivion.

PART III

THERE IS FEAR FROM ALL SIDES

Many Americans are frightened by what they believe is the specter of populism; other Americans are frightened by radical progressivism. Fear of American populism derives in large part from false analogies with mid-20th century fascism; fear of progressivism derives in part from its perceived mimicry of mid-20th century communism. The record of mid-20th century fascism and the record of mid-20th century communism are both brutal in the extreme. Thus, the past haunts our present, even when analogies are mistaken.

CHAPTER SEVEN

WILL POPULISTS PERSECUTE MINORITIES AND PLUNGE THE WORLD INTO WAR?

"Tear-it-all-down-populism!" So did *The New York Times* condemn populism on September 5, 2018. *The New York Times'* immediate reference was to populist attacks on the European Union, especially via Brexit. But it also was attacking what was said to be Trump's destruction of US military alliances. The critical label — *tear it down!* — could apply equally well to domestic populism in the eyes of its critics.

Populism is mis-portrayed as intolerant on a whole range of categories — racial, gender, sexual orientation, religious, political, and ethnic. Although discrimination is not now widespread by populists, it is feared by many that if populists gain increasing political power, discrimination will follow.

Straw-man populists are viewed as anti-intellectual. It is common for liberals and progressives to refer to populists as dumb and stupid, and to regard them as such.

Populist politicians are unjustifiably caricatured as dishonest — habitually lying to voters. It is common for leftists to shun all media considered populist-oriented. Many populists behave the same way, ignoring progressive media outlets. This behavior widens the divide in understanding between America's left and right.

American populist leaders, who are conspicuous by their invisibility with the sole exception of Trump, are disparaged as bellicose and adventurist abroad. Many fear that Trump will take the country to war.

Progressive commentaries and propaganda have made Trump the epitome of each of these anti-populist fears.

Populists Seen Lacking Compassion

Many leftists and moderates stereotype populists as lacking compassion for others. During the Trump presidency, this message has been driven in by media reporting on how immigrants are treated at our southern border, and attributing the behavior indiscriminately to populists. The media alleges that children are deliberately separated from their parents and housed in deplorable conditions. People who have been in our country for years as solid citizens are said to be suddenly arrested and deported. It alleges that refugees are denied admission to our country and sent back to intolerable conditions from the countries from which they came without sufficient justification.

The merits of these progressive and liberal claims are much disputed by the Administration, but they are accepted as fact by many Americans. The Administration and its supporters have been unable to put them to rest. Some Administration opponents suspect that Trump secretly welcomes the complaints because he believes he gains support among populists by appearing to be tough on immigrants.

Conservatives had a similar reputation during the George W. Bush Administration. Perceiving the reputation as a problem, Bush declared himself and his supporters to be "compassionate conservatives." He had recognized a problem and responded to it, whether or not successfully. There has been no attempt to define a compassionate Trump, or compassionate populists.

Ignoring the Dangers of Climate Change

At the top of the list of lies, populists are alleged to tell is their supposed denial of the dangers of climate change. Trump, and hence by inference, populists, are said to place current concerns about economic growth and jobs above dangers to the environment. The contention that populists oppose some environmentalist policies that jeopardize jobs and economic growth like a total ban on non-renewable fuels (petroleum, natural gas, and coal) is certainly true. Populists disbelieve many environmentalist "the sky is falling" claims about impending Armageddon and ordinarily prefer to maintain or revive jobs in industries targeted by climate change activists. Among progressives who believe there is imminent danger from rising temperatures, there is extreme frustration with populists over this issue and a panic about feared consequences.

It is not only populists' concern for the economy over the dangers of climate change that seems to be shortsighted to progressives. Populists also tend to be nationalists, in contrast to the internationalism of progressives. Progressives pride themselves on seeing the world as a whole — even romanticizing it as a personality, Gaia. They emphasize the interconnection of the natural forces of the planet. Melting ice in the Artic, flooded lowlands in the tropics. Changing atmospheric temperatures spawn violent storms all over the globe. The greatest dangers of climate change may be reducing the amount of arable land and so putting into motion large numbers of people.

"What," I asked a prominent environmentalist, "are you afraid of from global warming?" He replied, "The four horsemen of St. John's Apocalypse: war, famine, pestilence and death." That is, starvation will set in motion the movement of masses of people, struggles for livelihoods and even survival that will spawn migration, political turmoil, and war. Our country is likely better insulated from these consequences of climate change than other countries, but over time, the disruption in the world will impact us dramatically as well.

Progressives insist that opposition to their *save the earth* campaign is "racist and colonialist."

> After all, the climate crisis is not just about the environment. It is a crisis of human rights, of justice, and of political will. Colonial, racist, and patriarchal systems of oppression have created and fueled it. (Greta Thunberg, https://twitter.com/GretaThunberg/status/1200374750368976897)

Progressives are very concerned at this prospect and view populists as fatally myopic in their refusal to recognize and respond to the dangers.

In early October 2019, the Congressional sponsors of the so-called Green New Deal held a town hall discussion for the public at which a young woman declared that the earth had only a few more months of survival before climate change destroyed it, and that population growth was a central problem that should be stopped by people eating babies. No one could tell if she were serious or not. Since progressives support discretionary abortion (but not yet post-partum euthanasia), a proposal to kill and eat babies might be serious. In this episode, populist met progressive head-on. Populists think progressives are crazy to elicit such a proposal, and progressives think populists are irresponsible not to join in the fight against climate change before it is too late.

What is unfortunate is that a serious dialogue about climate change does not occur. Populists blame progressives for trying to stamp out opposing voices. Progressives blame populists for being stubbornly anti-scientific.

If a dialogue could take place — and our democratic political process is supposed to assure that one does take place in the Congress — populists would reply something like this:

> We are told in secret by top scientists that the scientific underpinnings of the progressive position are weak. The scientists who tell us this beg us not to reveal their names because they fear retaliation from progressives in their universities and in the public space. This is a consequence of the progressives' tendency to steamroll other people toward the progressive point of view in everything.

Progressives would reply at this point that there may be a few scientists who are outliers, but the great mass of scientific opinion supports the progressive position on climate change, and there are numerous papers, conferences, and petitions to show that.

Populists might then reply with a story. In the early 19th century when the first European explorers began to return from visiting central Africa, where the Equator bisects the continent, they were invited to relate their findings at a meeting of the Royal Geographic Society in London which had financed much of their travel. The returning explorers told large audiences, including most of the top scientists of the day, that they had seen mountains covered with snow in central Africa. These tales were greeted with noisy ridicule that immediately found its way into the press. Everyone knew that the climate was too hot at the Equator for there to be snow. The explorers were hounded out of town. Yet they were correct. Mounts Kilimanjaro and Kenya have snowcaps most of the year. It is not only latitude that matters to temperature but altitude — a very simple proposition for us today, but one that was unrecognized then. The lesson is that science is about being right; and right is not determined by the number of people who hold an opinion, even if they are experts. Science is not a political matter — issues are not properly settled by voting.

Progressives may be right that human carbon emissions are creating a crisis in our climate, but the matter requires scientific proof, not political pressure. This should be possible if the progressive position is defensible because scientific matters are often given to generally accepted proof, so it can be done. Populists say they can be convinced, but not stampeded.

Populists as Warmongers

Trump and, derivatively, American populists are viewed by their opponents as militaristic and adventuristic abroad — as war-like. Populist leaders are likely to take the country into war, it is feared. These fears were loudly and frequently voiced during the 2016 presidential campaign and during the first months of the Trump presidency. But now three years have passed with Trump in office, and other than a brief attack on a Syrian government airbase there has been no significant use of the military by President Trump. The President seems given to blustering threats aimed at other countries, with no military follow-up. Many people were stunned when Trump let pass both an Iranian attack on an American drone and then an Iranian (though Iran denies it) attack on the major Saudi oil field without military response. Trump almost appears a pacifist president. In consequence, attacks on Trump and his populist supporters from all other political directions (progressives, liberals, and conservatives) for being overly belligerent have all but stopped.

At various times during the last four years (2015–2019) progressive allegations and commentaries have made Trump the epitome of each of these fears. The charges are directed derivatively by casual inference at his base of populist voters as well.

Populists as Nazis

Much of the fear of populism arises out of remembrance of the atrocities of the Nazis in the 1930s and 1940s. The extreme fear of populism that many people display has no basis in what American populists are now doing. The fear is entirely focused on what they may do or are going to do. The nurturing of this fear has been part of America's and Europe's political landscape since the end of World War II. (See Alfred Hitchcock's film, *Not*, 1946.)

It is common for critics of populism to tar it with the brush of Nazism and fascism. The German Nazis were in fact brutally intolerant of all the categories of people listed above — based on racial, gender, sexual orientation, religious, political, and ethnic differences. In America, people in these categories believe that they have made striking progress in public acceptance and lessened discrimination in recent decades, and many see populism as an effort to reverse that progress.

The identification of modern populism with Hitler's Nazism is a polemic overreach. The right of the political spectrum has more elements than populism, such as its lunatic fringe — the neo-Nazis. Neo-Nazis, like the Hitlerites themselves, used much rhetoric which is echoed by today's populism. Nazis then and now were nationalists and spoke of the nation as a family and praised national traditions. American populists today use some of the same language.

But, unlike today's populists, Nazis gave a distinctly ethnic and racist flavor to their nationalism. That is missing, at least overtly, in today's American populism, although Trump himself is routinely accused of racism, Islamophobia, and misogyny. Critics of mainstream America and, by extension, populism, insist that it is there in a disguised fashion and point to code words and symbols as evidence of this. Perhaps there is an element of truth in this. It would not be a surprise. Racism has a long and continuing history in America. There is evidence, however, that despite the continual condemnation of racism by the left, it does continue to have a footprint there, especially in Ilhan Omar and the Britain's Labor Party (virulent anti-Semitism). The same is true of sexism. Many of the most dramatic cases of sexual harassment which have been publicized in recent years in America have been the work of people who have declared themselves liberals, socialists, communists, and progressives.

Populists and fascists are not the same thing. Nazis were not 1930s populists. If a reader of this book thinks today's populists are Nazis, it is likely because of media framing. It is because the progressive and liberal anti-populists have suggested it via the media.

There are clear and valid reasons for being anti-establishment as populists are. One need not be a Nazi to be anti-establishment, as in fact progressives show.

But the accusation that populists are Nazis is a harsh one and rankles. More than 300,000 Americans lost their lives in World War II, many fighting the Nazis. To be accused of being Nazis because of populist political leaning causes some, and may in time cause many more, populists to conclude that if one is to be damned falsely, one might as well adopt some of the condemned attributes. For example, Nazis had quasi-military units. Progressives have them today. Perhaps populists would benefit from having them as well.

Neo-Nazis are not part of the populist movement. The pro-fascist group has a political agenda of its own. Unlike populism, it is not basically anti-establishment.

American populists generally denounce neo-Nazis. Progressivists do not denounce anti-fa. There is no symmetry between the two movements in this. Today in America, progressives have a small but active armed wing — anti-fa, but the populists have nothing of the sort.

It is something of a surprise that populism has no militant wing today in the United States. The SS and the SA (Nazi paramilitary organizations) were large and defining elements of Nazism in Germany.

So large were the SA (the Brownshirts), for example, that one of the most important agreements which Hitler made on attaining power in Germany was to agree with the German Army that he would not replace it (the German Army) with the SA. The SA was supposed to shrink over time. Hitler kept this agreement.

The Progressive Attitude Toward Populism

[There is now] a far more destructive and potentially genocidal ethno-nationalism, the ferocity of which is fueled by economic disparity, religious intolerance and retrograde ideologies regarding gender, race and sexuality. The possible global futures we face are fearful…. (The International Academic Forum (IAFOR), *Call for Papers: The Asian Conference on Asian Studies 2018*, November 8, 2017.)

The sentences above are characterizations of populism. They make it clear that the criticisms of populism are international in scope because they were penned by a Japanese author.

Note that the old socialist effort to assist the common people — Lenin–Stalin's *socialism in one country* — is now described by the left as ethno-nationalist and genocidal. Populism is an attempt to assist the common people in the working and middle class. It is now denounced by progressives. We might ask, the attempt to help America's forgotten yeoman is genocidal to …. whom? The ruling classes? Those who are dependent on the labor of the common people without working themselves — the nepotistic establishment and the recipients of government largess? It is interesting to see populism's espousal of what used to be leftist doctrines now denounced by the left in these harsh terms.

CHAPTER EIGHT

WILL PROGRESSIVES OPPRESS
THEIR OPPONENTS?

Populists and progressives are both strongly anti-establishment. Populists oppose the joint conservative, liberal, and progressive establishment. Progressives only oppose the establishment's liberal, conservative and populist elements — not even Trump is part of the establishment. Populists and progressives share a key common attitude toward conservatives and liberals. In an imagined dialogue, populists might say to progressives, "We support many of the same things you do, but we think you are riding the wrong horse to get them because progressive leaders will do nothing for you, and because their tactics are destructive of our nation and its values."

The deepening division of the American electorate into hostile political camps — populists and progressives — has increased the level of political fear in America dramatically. Decades ago, politics was a sort of sport of disagreement in America. The two parties — Democrats and Republicans — were both near to the center of the political spectrum and could cooperate with each other. In the country, Democrats and Republicans argued with each other, but often remained friends.

All that is gone now. Politics is more like a blood sport with deep animosities and advantage taken of the other side whenever possible.

Once, when Donald Trump was running for president in 2016, I (Mills) was invited, because I knew him personally, to meet with a group of professors at Harvard to answer their question, "What is going on?"

I tried to explain the rise of populism in the Midwest and South as best as I could, and to explain Trump's attraction to voters in those regions. I had known the people at the lunch table for decades. But as I spoke, my tone infuriated some of them. I was not denouncing Trump. I was discussing him as if he were an ordinary human being with strengths and weaknesses. Finally, unable to bear his outrage any longer, one of the group (a distinguished man who was author of several books, whose father and grandfather had been US Senators, and who had himself run unsuccessfully for the Senate, a Republican by party affiliation) stood up, angrily denounced not Trump, but me — for daring to speak as if Donald Trump were an ordinary person with strengths and weaknesses and not an entirely disreputable character about whom nothing normal could be found. My friend could not stand to hear Trump *normalized*. He then stomped out of the room. That was the end of what had been a long friendship.

Incidents like this are occurring all over the nation now. Friends are insulting friends. Friendships are breaking up. Family members no longer talk to one another. To maintain relationships, people avoid any political discussions. It is common for people to conceal their political leanings from others.

Populists fear progressives, and progressives fear the straw-man populists. Progressives fear (unjustly) that populists hate minority groups and will discriminate against them if allowed to. Populists fear that progressives hate them, that is, populists (or as progressives refer to them, *deplorables*), and will discriminate against them in whatever ways are possible. Both sides fear character assassination and false claims by the other.

Progressive zealots view their opponents not as people who can be persuaded to switch sides, but as bigots, racists, exploiters, and enemies of decent people. They attack them personally, often without factual bases, and justify these things by the end they are intended to serve — the victory of the progressive revolution.

Populists who think deeply join with conservatives to fear that progressivism is a late stage in the decadence of modern culture, stretching back to the French Revolution. They see modern art and much literature and theatre as absurd and undermining public attitudes from constructive to deconstructive (to use the jargon of the left). Progressivism seems to them the translation of decadence into the political sphere. People on the right who know history can visualize themselves as Romans watching the flood of barbarism overwhelm the Roman Empire. They know it ended badly for the Romans and fear it will end badly for themselves in our era.

Progressives seem to be caught in large-scale inconsistencies. They seem bent on criminalizing much speech (political correctness) and much of ordinary political behavior — such as gathering dirt on competitors — especially when it can be charged to Republicans. But progressives also seem bent on decriminalizing what have been felonies — in particular breaking and entering, theft, and assault — so that in Democrat-run cities, police no longer investigate these crimes or file charges, and citizens seem increasingly at the mercy of rough elements of the population. Populists, conservatives, and many moderates are afraid for their own safety in cities and states that are run by progressives, and in the nation itself should it fall into the direction of progressives.

How Populists and Others Fear the Motives of Progressives

Populists and moderates fear progressives for the same reason progressives give for fearing Trump — that progressives want only to grasp power for their own purposes. Others fear that progressives intend to exploit power to attain wealth and other advantages for themselves, and progressivism is only the rhetoric they use to gain election to office. The extensive benefits and entitlements proffered by progressives are not believed to be real because they are not believed to be feasible (they are too costly or too disruptive of ordinary life) and so they are seen as dishonest and false. Where distrust is this deep, no amount of discussion or debate serves to lessen it — instead, people tend to talk past one another, each adhering to a pre-conceived narrative that has no place to let the other side enter.

Conservatives wonder who is paying the raft of lawyers representing whistle-blowers who are objecting to President Trump's actions. The whistle-blower concept was intended, conservatives thought, to make it possible for people of low rank who knew big secrets to go outside lines of command to tell those responsible who had authority so they could make it right. Now whistle-blowers lawyer up with teams of high-cost attorneys to write their messages in formal, lengthy petitions to present to the Congress. The whistle-blower process has been weaponized in political contests by the progressives.

They Fear the Excesses of Multi-Culturalism

It is common among progressives to insist that all cultures are on the same basis. Art is of equal value from wherever it comes and of whatever it consists (a specious argument vetted partly to create an artificially favorable museum market for radical feminist and minority artists). The work of individual artists can be evaluated against that of other artists and judgments made, but cultural differences carry no significance — one is as good as another.

Critics of progressivism are inclined to acknowledge that there can be good in the artistic and other expressions of different cultures, but they also believe that progressive multi-culturalism goes too far. In architecture, for example, the hut for worship of a nature deity in the village of a nomadic tribe is not comparable to a Gothic cathedral; the outsize hut of a tribal monarch is not comparable to Versailles. In essence, critics insist that there are standards of quality that progressives seem determined to ignore.

They Fear for Freedom of Thought and Speech

"Marxism is the opium of the intellectuals," Raymond Aron said of Marxism in 1955 (Raymond Aron, *The Opium of the Intellectuals*, Paris: Calmann-Lévy, 1955). Populists are not alone in seeing a deep strain of Marxism in modern American progressivism. Marxism has long been the opiate of intellectuals and is a wellspring for entitlement socialist ideas including entitlement, affirmative action, and restorative justice. Those who do not agree are denounced as riffraff.

The insistence of the left on political correctness in word and deed causes non-leftists to fear for their freedom of thought and expression. There are many examples of how political correctness is enforced and why it is therefore of concern to non-leftists. The most glaring example of limitations on free speech are found on college campuses. We cite a recent one here.

> A team at the University of Michigan at Ann Arbor that helps students who feel they've been harassed or bullied uses "implicit threat of punishment and intimidation to quell speech," a federal appeals court ruled this week.
>
> A student whose speech is seen by another student as hurtful to his or her feelings may receive a knock on the door from a team of school officials threatening to refer the student for discipline unless he or she submits to "restorative justice," "individualized education," or "unconscious bias training," students aggrieved by the approach told the court. They added to the court that "[students] enrolled at Michigan steer clear of discussing topics including immigration, identity politics, and abortion for fear they might be anonymously reported to the bias team for "offensive, biased, and/or hateful" speech, the group wrote.
>
> The University of Michigan defended its actions. The University argued that it was fine to operate what appear to be peer-pressure patrols. To those who are or might be the victims of this approach, it appears to be thought control based on political correctness.
>
> Further, a Federal District Court had approved this mechanism of repressive thought control, and it wasn't rejected as illegal under the First Amendment to the Constitution which guarantees free speech until it reached the Appellate Court level, just shy of the US Supreme Court. (Katherine Mangan, "Michigan's Bias-Response Team Uses Indirect Threats to Chill Free Speech, Appeals Court Finds," *Chronicle of Higher Education*, September 25, 2019.)

It cannot be expected that efforts like this will be limited to universities if progressives gain national power.

There are many other ways that universities impose thought and speech control, and some are so subtle that they are not challenged in courts. In particular, the First Amendment is turned against freedom of speech by the use of petitions. Petitions are drafted which reflect the position of progressives on current political issues — for example, supporting late-term abortion, or the impeachment of President Trump. The petitions are circulated by hand or online. A person is told that he or she does not have to sign them, but if he or she does not sign, then he or she is identified as not with the progressives and is subjected to many forms of retribution. Professors are fired for what are said to be other reasons or given back assignments and pushed to resign and go elsewhere, or subject to blacklisting in their fields or among schools so that they do not get opportunities to present their research or cannot find a job elsewhere. Staff persons who fail to toe the progressive line are fired for what are said to be other reasons or not promoted. Students are given lower grades than they earn and lose opportunities to supplement their learning by projects and travel. All — professors, staff and students — are subject to ostracism by the progressives who dominate the schools. Some people are sent to what are informal re-education camps in which sensitivity to others — following a progressive political line — is taught. A knowledgeable reader will think immediately of George Orwell's "thought police," or of Mao Zedong's three-in-one (workers, party, military) obligatory self-criticism indoctrination groups.

Direct action outside academia is used to suppress speakers, books, and movies when campus pressures do not suffice. Commonly a church or other venue for a talk will receive a message that says something like, "We wish no harm to your church. However, we cannot allow fascism to continue to rise and will not tolerate its presence in our city. We will shut down your showing of a propaganda film."

They Fear Favoritism for Favored Groups and Discrimination Against Themselves

People who are in favor of greater human diversity in our institutions and those who oppose more unmerited inclusion are both likely to fear the favoritism which progressives express for favored demographic groups. It appears that diversity and inclusion (quotas and preferences) which began as recommended routes to advancement for women and minorities have become ends in themselves. They then become a reason to set aside things which are equally or more important to other people — competence, knowledge, commitment, merit, performance, etc. When this happens, places of responsibility and reward threaten to become filled not with people of potential contribution but with time-servers of the favored demographic group. Also, more qualified (except politically) people are set aside, and they and their family, friends, and supporters are unhappy with this result.

They Fear for Religion

Progressivism is strongly anti-religious, with the sole exception of Islamic sensibilities (a reflection of its anti-colonialist sympathies). It shares with Marx the conviction that "religion (now including Buddhism because of Aung San Suu Kyi's stance on the civil status of Myanmar's Rohingya inhabitants) is the opium of the masses." It blames many of the horrors of history — including war, intolerance, bigotry, genocide — on organized religion, especially on Christianity. It opposes traditional morality whose sponsors it sees in the churches.

In consequence, non-Muslim religious Americans (Protestants, Catholics, Eastern Orthodox, Mormons, Confucians, Taoists, Hindus, Jains, Buddhists, and Jews), to whom religion is important, fear that progressives repress them. For example, Democratic candidate for president, Beto O'Rourke, is quoted as saying in the summer of 2019, "There can be no reward, no benefit, no tax break, for anyone or any institution, any organization in America that denies the full human rights and the full civil rights of every single one of us." O'Rourke refers by his expression to "the full civil rights of every single one of us" on such issues as gay marriage, which is opposed in many religious communities. Non-progressives fear that behind this sort of moral/political mix lies intolerance for religion.

They Fear Self-Hatred

Many people worry about the self-deprecation progressives try to impose on whites of European ancestry. The universities teach the gospel of white guilt and privilege. The notions are that, in America, white people are privileged in many ways above others and that they should atone for it by supporting progressivism.

To progressives, it must be strange to discover that many people of European descent do not feel themselves privileged. The large numbers of whites who support populism are frustrated by their gradual impoverishment and certainly do not think themselves privileged. From their perspective some whites are privileged, but most are not. Labeling all whites privileged is absurd and insulting.

Nor do all whites, perhaps only a small number, feel shame for their history in America and countries of origin. Yes, there were violent and brutal things done in the conquest of the Americas. Yes, they say, it would have been better if those things had not happened. Nonetheless, what has emerged from those events are the nations of the Americas today — especially the United States. The progressives who so bitterly criticize whites also benefit enormously from what the Europeans built in America — and progressives, from this perspective, are simply trying to misappropriate the fruits of the common people's labor.

They Fear Damage from Falsified History

There are people for whom trying to get the facts of history right is important. They believe that an accurate understanding of our past is key to a successful navigation of our future.

The progressive's method of falsifying history is clever. The information given is not always wrong; mostly it is misleadingly incomplete. With key evidence intentionally omitted, a false narrative is made persuasive to a gullible student. The method is to use not overt lies, but half-truths. The result is that people of European descent are made ashamed of their ancestors. They are made guilt-ridden and exhorted to atone. Yet, populists argue, the ordinary Europeans created the Americas of today in which all of us live and many, including many progressives and liberals, prosper. The progressives do not propose to expel whites from the Americas, only to use their half-true historical narratives for opportunistic political gain today.

The incomplete narrative, with key elements left out — the half-truth — is also a favorite journalistic device of progressives. It is not limited to them, of course.

A final tactic of which populists accuse progressives is accusing others of their own actions. It is another tactic developed honed by the Nazi/Communist regimes of the mid-20th century. By accusing the other side of what they are doing themselves, they muddy the water of responsibility, make their own crimes seem less dramatic, and damage the reputation of their opponents.

Progressives seem to have the same disrespect for current history, that which we call news, as they do for past history. They fake it in pursuit of their political objectives. This is not to say that others do not falsify news — they do. But since progressives insist that they do not create fake news, it is worth pointing out that they do. Progressives make a big thing of telling Americans that progressives tell them the truth (fact-checking). For example, the *New York Times* declares continually in its advertising that it provides "the truth."

Generally, when some media tells you it is telling the truth, it is lying. The official paper of the Soviet Communist Party was called *Pravda* (Truth). Once when I (Mills) was visiting the Soviet Union, a Soviet official told me that each morning he would listen to the *Voice of America* (an illegal act in the USSR) to learn what had happened in the world, and then read *Pravda* to get the Communist party line about it. In other words, he read *Pravda* for spin — the same reason knowledgeable people read the *New York Times* — to discover the progressive party line in America.

They Fear Socialism

The utopias promised by revolutionary entitlement socialism, and more recently by progressives, have more often than not ended with whimpers rather than bangs. Entitlement and revolutionary Marxist socialists have had ample opportunities over the past 250 years to experiment with government controls. As many experiments as there have been, so have there been as many failures. Only contemporary European democratic socialism can claim some success. Perhaps, Xi Jinping's Chinese market communism may someday prove to be another exception, but it still far from a paragon of egalitarianism and social justice.

Each time one socialist variety fails, true believers give their hearts to another. If they kept track of their failures, and the hundred plus millions of excess deaths in their experiments in the Soviet Union, China, Eastern Europe, North Korea, Cambodia, and elsewhere, many of them might find it difficult to go on.

Instead, they just block out all inconvenient aspects of the past and continue to seek political power. They ignore the downside in what they do. Today, it is particularly troubling that they disregard the greatly enhanced repressive capability that the internet is providing to authoritarian regimes (of which the communist regime in China is today's most extensive exploiter) and the capacity to hack into our secrets. Progressives and entitlement socialists seem to have no comprehension of how the future will turn out, so they make it up out of their own desires, and it is wholly an illusion. They live in fantasy worlds, both domestically and in foreign relations.

CHAPTER NINE

THE MITTERAND RULE

It is common now for progressive politicians to make what appear to some people to be extravagant promises in pursuit of elected office. For example, free *Cadillac* medical care is promised for all; a *comfortable* monthly allowance is promised for all; a *good* guaranteed job; free college tuition. To some people these are delusions because they are unaffordable to middle class taxpayers who inevitably foot the bill, and they believe that the progressive politicians making the promises know that the promises are onerous and electorally unfulfillable. If this is true, then the politicians making the promises are simply pandering in pursuit of office. This frightens many people because it suggests the decline of our elections into bidding wars with no link to reality. If the country goes down such a path, the result is likely to be calamitous. Hence, the apparent political dishonesty of progressive leaders frightens many non-progressives.

To make matters worse, *dreams* are mis-portrayed as moral imperatives. Progressives insist that medical care is a fundamental human right; so is higher education. As such, a just society must provide them to all its citizens and at affordable cost, or even free. Yet a moment's reflection suggests these proposals are not serious. People can have free medical care, but not at top-quality levels and not with all the newest drugs and procedures. There are cost and capacity constraints that always go unmentioned.

A decade or so ago, the then President of France, Francois Mitterand — an entitlement socialist who was the most-elected President of France — was asked by an aide what was the most important attribute of a successful politician. He replied something like, "I regret that I cannot say that it is honesty or courage, or something like that. But in truth, it is merely indifference." That is, Mitterand was saying, a politician must be able to shift positions quickly and completely, and to make this possible, indifference to the results of policy and events is most valuable. The politician must not appear indifferent, of course, rather, he or she must appear to be caring.

This is the Mitterand Rule: politicians should be indifferent to the consequences of the causes they champion.

Progressive politicians are especially good at this. For example, Senator Warren in her campaign for the presidency attacks large firms, threatening to break them up and to tax them and their owners and executives heavily. Yet many of those same firms and owners and executives support her candidacy. The media mention this as a paradox. Yet it clearly indicates that the targets of Senator Warren's attacks do not think she is serious about them, and believe that if she elected, she will play ball with them. They believe that if Warren is successful, she will abide by the Mitterand Rule. By midsummer 2019, in the heat of the contest for the Democratic presidential nomination, Senator Bernie Sanders was accusing candidate Senator Elizabeth Warren of being a capitalist driven by greed. He was accusing her of being a *faux* progressive.

On a larger scale, progressives proclaim their allegiance to the cause of making democracy better, as if they really intend to abide by the majority rule of liberals, conservatives, and populists. In pursuit of this noble ideal, they call for abolishing the electoral college and replacing it with majority winner-take-all balloting. This high-minded goal, however, is flagrantly contradicted by numerous anti-democratic planks in the progressive platform.

For example, the *resistance* to Trump's holding office which was proclaimed by progressives after Trump's election has only one other counterpart in American history when an effort was made to prevent a duly elected president taking office. It involved the efforts to assassinate Lincoln on his way to Washington, D.C. to be sworn in as president early in 1861. To argue that Trump was not a fairly elected president because he didn't win the popular vote is to reject his presidency on grounds that did not then, and do not now, exist — the American Constitution still provides for the choice of a president by an electoral college.

The resistance was and is a progressive effort. Liberals do not behave that way. For example, faced with a virtually tied presidential election, Al Gore conceded the election and made no suggestion of a resistance to George W. Bush's assuming the presidency. Even the progressive's favorite demon (until Trump), Richard Nixon, had done something similar in conceding the election in 1960 to John F. Kennedy. Liberals and conservatives have too much concern for the stability of American government to endanger it with calls for resistance to an elected president.

Progressives do not. This fact is deeply disturbing to many people about progressivism.

Populists Fear a Lack of Patriotism

Many Americans are patriots. They honor the symbols of the nation — its flag, its national anthem, its pledge to the flag. They honor veterans of our wars — many are veterans or families of veterans. They honor those killed in our wars. They honor our police and police-like officers.

In progressivism, they see a very different attitude. They see people who view the United States as a proponent of slavery, colonialism, and war. Progressives denounce our Declaration of Independence with its stirring statements such as "All men are created equal" as hypocrisy. They disrespect the symbols of the nation and call for a full revision of its governing documents and a revision of its history as taught in schools and honored in our public life.

The narrative about Europeans destroying high civilizations in the Americas during the age of discovery and conquest feeds into a worldview disturbing to non-progressives.

Progressives often appear to be unpatriotic — to despise the United States as it was and is. The blemishes on American history — slavery in particular, but also the destruction of the native American tribes, the lengthy exploitation of labor by businesses, and American support for repressive regimes abroad — seem in progressive eyes to be the primary story of American history. They disrespect the symbols of the nation.

Support for the military is minimal — progressives do not enlist in the military and do not support its activities abroad. These attitudes are deeply troubling to populists and conservatives who pride themselves on their loyalty and respect for the nation and its symbols.

Many non-progressives find the progressive credo repellent, frightening and threatening.

They Fear a Society Overrun with Crime

Liberals and progressives, after discovering that disproportionate numbers of African-Americans were incarcerated, sought to rectify the perceived injustice by reducing the numbers of African-Americans arrested and jailed. Liberals and progressives also discovered that police sometimes treated African-Americans brutally. They tried to mitigate the problem by minimizing police interaction with African-Americans. They made progress. Arrests for offenses like burglary are falling at a rapid rate. No one maintains that crime rates are falling. Police simply no longer investigate many complaints.

Democratic presidential candidates are attempting to outdo each other with suggested *magic bullet* changes. For example, Former Vice President Biden has called for no jail time for non-violent crimes. This is not a liberal proposition. It is a progressive one and shows Biden, along with other liberals, adopting progressive proposals.

Many non-progressives fear that America is becoming a safe haven for criminals.

They Fear Financial Disaster

Populists worry about the fiscal irresponsibility of progressives. Nancy Pelosi denounced the Trump tax cuts as crumbs for the middle class — she was right, compared to the radical promises the Democrats are making — free healthcare, free college tuition, etc. It is fair to say that American presidential campaigns have become bidding wars. The left promises expensive benefit programs (except for conservatives and populists); the right promises expensive tax cuts (disproportionately benefiting conservatives). The federal budget deficit (and thus federal borrowing) now substantially exceeds one trillion dollars a year. Some populists and some progressives worry about the buildup of federal debt — now 15 percent greater than the entire output of the American economy in a single year. Populists insist it is the high bidding of progressive politicians for votes that forces the nation to abandon fiscal responsibility. "You are forcing us to drive the country into financial disaster," populists charge, "because if we propose cutbacks in spending the electorate will abandon us for you. We would do better both to moderate our spending."

Finally, populists and many conservatives fear that progressive policies will kill the goose that lays the golden eggs — that is, the American economy. They fear that higher income tax rates, a new wealth tax, and nationalization of healthcare (about one-fifth of our entire economy), and proposals to break up large firms will be counter-productive.

CHAPTER TEN

IS THERE A PLACE TO HIDE?

Many people still think that there is a big and cautious middle in the American electorate that is uncomfortable with political extremes — with both populists and progressives. Republicans are especially susceptible to this belief, but they are not alone. They believe the political party that appeals most effectively to the middle will win the 2020 election. Joe Biden's campaign for the Democratic presidential nomination has been very much based on the notion that he can appeal to the big middle in the American electorate because he gives the appearance of being a cautious and likeable person.

Where has the middle of the American electorate been in the past? It has been in small towns and suburbs, on the farms and in the family-owned stores — on the conservative side — and in the factories and on the roads, in the unions — on the liberal side. These venues, however, have eroded. America is now highly urbanized with an emotional and fickle electorate. On the conservative side, family farms and shops have given way to large corporations, and unions have declined greatly in importance, as have blue-collar jobs generally.

Nor do polls show a large and stable political middle. Instead, polls show broad dissatisfaction with both major political parties and with the national government generally.

There are now wings to our electorate populated by radicals and zealots. Radicalism lies in the eyes of the beholder. To populists, the progressives are radical. To progressives, the populists are radical.

To conservatives, both populists and progressives are radical. To liberals, both conservatives and populists are radicals.

Populists and progressives have each chosen sides in the political controversies of our time. They listen to or read with respect only materials which are from the side they have chosen. If they listen to or read anything from the other side, it is with head-shaking disagreement and even anger. They are not open to persuasion.

A core characteristic of the middle of the electorate in the past was that it was open to argument from politicians on both sides. There was a large independent thinking middle which often decided election contests. There is a remnant of that today, but it seems small.

Many people cannot accept or even consider what others say. This is so even if they appear to listen.

A populist is a populist not because he or she is convinced by populist spokespersons; instead, they are convinced because they have already adopted the populist position. They listen to populist propaganda exclusively and accept it fully, although it is more difficult for populists to do this because liberal and progressive propaganda dominate the media.

Essentially the same is true of progressives — that is, progressives are progressives not because they are convinced by arguments, but because they already accept the progressive position. The big exception is young people who are still open to persuasion by either side until they adopt a political orientation and close their minds to alternative points of view.

We do not know how people become populists or progressives before keeping themselves that way by closing their minds to other points of view. There may be many paths to becoming a committed populist or progressive. A person may follow his or her parents' orientation, may choose an orientation because of his or her demographic identity, or may experience an economic advantage at some point in one or the other political side. Nonetheless, whatever the origin of a person's orientation, for more and more people, it becomes rigid.

We do not have reliable statistics on the numbers of Americans who are populists or progressives. Our statistics on liberals and conservatives are far more reliable. This is largely because the terms liberal and conservative are understood well enough that people can identify with one or the other. The terms populist and progressive are fuzzier, so people cannot reliably identify themselves with one or the other.

It matters that we do not have reliable measures of the number of progressives and populists in our population because these two groups are coming to drive our political processes.

An important dividing line between radical and moderate is the attitude each takes toward conflict resolution.

Progressives have a zero-sum mentality. They treat others as enemies and fight to the death. Theirs is a value-subtracting game. Kill the enemy regardless of the cost to your own side. True progressives do not compromise. Conservatives, by contrast are often practical and will compromise to attain some of an objective, but rigid conservatives, like progressives, do not compromise. Sometimes progressives will pretend to compromise, but this is always simply a tactic — a New Economic Policy-era Leninist steps back before taking two steps forward when opportunity knocks.

Liberals advocate personal choice and voluntary exchange to generate prosperity (value-added) and efficiently distribute income. Their mentality favors accommodation and prosperity over do-or-die causes. Populists, like liberals, are willing to compromise to make progress. This is especially true regarding economics, governance, and foreign policy issues, with one exception. Many pro-lifers are populists, and Trump, as a populist president, has supported the extreme pro-life position. For many pro-lifers, the pro-life position is absolute and non-negotiable. To moderates, the abortion controversy appears relatively easy to compromise into a working solution and allow the nation's political attention to turn to other pressing matters. A compromise would permit early-term abortion at a woman's choice, and prohibit late-term abortion except when the mother's life is in danger. However, neither pro-lifers nor progressive pro-choicers will accept such a compromise — both instead insist on the absolute terms of their positions.

Politicians, like Trump, choose to ride one horse (pro-life in his case) or another (pro-choice in the case of all Democrat leaders). Remember the Mitterand Rule — successful politicians do not care about the issues. They pick an issue to support because the people who really care about that issue then contribute money and physical assistance to the politicians' campaigns. Politicians and true believers — pro-lifers or pro-choicers — prefer endless political controversy to practical accommodation. Pro-lifers and pro-choicers want to fight it out forever. Both sides benefit from unending controversy. Politicians gain campaign support and votes; true believers do not have to surrender any of their moral position. The result is that aspects of the battle end up in the Supreme Court which cannot amicably resolve them, and each Court decision is measured as a win for one side and a loss for the other.

With the major exception of the abortion issue, populists are willing to compromise. It is the firmly ideological conservative true believers and, unlikely bed-fellows, the far-right, neo-Nazi radicals and progressives who are unwilling to compromise. Politics involves strange similarities and this is one. Liberals and populists are akin to moderates in being willing to compromise; progressives, conservatives and neo-Nazis are alike in being unwilling to compromise and insisting that it is their way or the highway. It is the increasing significance of progressives in our political life that is making compromise less and less achievable.

The establishment is conflicted because it favors win–win solutions such as free trade and personal liberty, but at the same time sympathizes with the die-hard *entitlement social justice* crowd. While, the liberal establishment talks accommodation, it is tempted to act the other way.

Progressives are *social justice warriors*. They relish the battle. Populists prefer compromise. They want tranquility and prosperity. In the older literature progressives were called *irrationalists* because they rejected rational choice. Populists were *rationalists* who set limits on their passions.

The demands made by progressives are usually non-negotiable. Hence, confrontation, not dialogue, is often inevitable. Non-negotiable demands incline progressives toward repression.

Socialists, especially those in the liberal establishment, are doubleminded. They want to liberate the oppressed for the common good, and stifle them to deter incorrect behavior. This is why many people intuitively fear the duplicity of socialist politicians. They perceive entitlement socialists as wolves in sheep clothing, peaceful on the outside and vicious on the inside.

Being insistent seems admirable to some people. Compromising seems admirable to others. In America today, progressives are unwilling and populists are willing to compromise.

If there were a substantial middle of the American electorate, then it might be hoped that it would serve as a balance wheel to our political process, but even then prospects would be dim because the information that is available to the public is now largely partisan and ideological. The mass media, including social media, presents information that is often false (fake news) and always spun (given a biased interpretation).

It is a great illusion of the Anglo-Saxon world that a neutral person, like a judge or a jury, can take two special pleadings and determine the facts from them. I (Mills) have served as a judge for some 20 years. It is not possible for a neutral person to make truth out of two lies. The truth does not necessarily lie between two false extremes, nor can it be constructed out of false information.

To make the system work well, witnesses and attorneys have to tell the truth. Then a judge can often construct a reasonably accurate narrative of what really happened and apply the law to that. However, if witnesses and attorneys feel free to invent a narrative that is favorable to them, judges and juries are misled. For example, a jury is supposed to decide which of two conflicting witnesses is more credible — that is, telling the truth. If both are lying, what is the jury to do?

I was a private judge. My decisions were subject to review by federal courts. I decided to quit taking cases when the opposing attorneys in some of my cases came to me after I had rendered a decision and said to me, "Now, let us tell you what really happened." Their witnesses had felt free to lie; and they, the attorneys, had felt free to rely on the lies in constructing arguments. Penalty of perjury is supposed to compel witnesses to tell the truth. In today's America, it is generally ineffective.

I realized that the decisions I was making were largely nonsense because I lacked enough truth to work with. I was ashamed of many of my decisions and quit judging cases.

Centrists in America face the same predicament. Seeking to act sensibly in their political decisions, they need enough truthful information, but do not get it. Progressives control most of the media and they do not tell the truth. They only provide snippets of it. Conservatives have a small part of the mass media, but they also falsify and spin. There is an inadequate basis of truth for independents to work with. So even if there were a significant middle in the American electorate, it would be misled by a wilderness of lies.

The danger feared by the moderate center of our political spectrum, no matter what its size, is that the populists or progressives as they pursue power will come to get us. We will no longer be able to escape the political turmoil.

PART IV

WHY RADICALIZATION
IS HAPPENING

Something as complex as the change which is occurring in the American political landscape has many causes. It can be studied from multiple perspectives. In the next two chapters we consider the economic and generational causes, as we believe them to be of major importance.

CHAPTER ELEVEN

DOMESTIC DISINTEGRATION

I run a small business — a gas station. I have pumps and hoses that are fully up to code. Then the government changes the code and I have to replace them. Six months later, it changes the code back and I have to replace them again. Every six years I have to replace the storage tanks for the gas which is an enormous expense for me. And the inspectors are here every week about something or other. And I have to fill out the same business tax returns for the federal and state governments that the huge corporations have to fill out. It's almost impossible to run a small business.

The person who made that complaint is the epitome of the populist voter. He is an ordinary guy seeking a better deal in life and his great enemy is the government. He is told by the establishment that the United States is rated the most business-friendly in the world. He is told by the progressives that he is an enemy of the environment and that he should be out of business. The liberals want him to clean up his act, at more cost to him. The conservatives praise him, but they get nothing done for him. For the small business owner, the progressives are simply enemies. He fears that to progressives he is what the kulaks were to the Soviets in the 1920s — a class of people which should be eliminated. The Soviets eliminated the kulaks by execution, forced labor, and starvation. The progressives would eliminate small business people by government over-regulation.

Liberals, conservatives, and the big government establishment are not this man's friends. This explains why he is a populist.

No matter how hard I work, no matter how long I work, no matter how many jobs I work, I just can't seem to get ahead. Whatever more I might make is absorbed in increasing healthcare costs and rising prices. The government says that there is almost no inflation, but I pay more for basics all the time. Maybe if you don't try to get ahead, but just live at the same low standard you've been living, then it doesn't cost more. But I sure can't get ahead.

The person who told me this was an employee in a pharmacy. He also has become a populist.

The income of ordinary people is now consumed in living expenses so that they have almost no savings. Most people borrow to make ends meet. A great deal of borrowing is in the form of credit card debt and interest is charged at rates that used to be considered usury and were illegal. Surveys say that the great majority of the American population could not find 400 dollars to meet an unexpected emergency. Medical expenses pose a threat of financial ruin to most Americans who simply live in the hope that a medical emergency will not occur.

Somewhat more than half the adults in the United States, those on the lower half of the income ladder, have been left out of the economic growth of the American economy since the 1970s. Real wages in America have been flat for more than four decades. They have not prospered and they are certain that their children will not do better than they have done. Their children are also pessimistic about the future. The notion that children will live better than parents is a key part of what has been called the American Dream. Its abandonment by millions of Americans reflects a deep disillusionment.

When I (Mills) was helping run the American economy for the federal government during the 1960s and 1970s, the rule of thumb was that the CEO of a company would make 40 times the earnings of the average employee. Today that number is about 300 times.

The rise of China is a great thing. However, American leadership let it be done at the expense of the American worker. They made no accommodation for him/her. They abandoned and then insulted them. Populism is the direct result.

President Ronald Reagan accelerated the export of American manufacturing jobs abroad. The deep economic causes were the evolution of the Japanese into high-quality manufacturers with strong retail presence in America. This had been developing since the end of World War II when Japanese goods exported to America were renowned for being cheap and of low quality. During the 1970s and 1980s it was remarkable to many of us at the Harvard Business School how American auto manufacturers in particular continued to focus on their rivalry with each other and ignored the steady erosion of their domestic market by Japanese competitors. The developing strength of Japanese exporters to America was followed by the emergence of manufacturing capability in China, then in other Asian nations. In effect, hundreds of millions of new workers at low (by American standards) wages had entered the world's labor force and employers with government support were figuring out how to utilize them to challenge American manufacturers in the United States itself.

Resistance to these developments would have required an industrial policy in the United States aimed at preserving American jobs. This was not forthcoming. In part, the American unions, which would have been likely spearheads of such a policy, were being weakened dramatically by employer efforts and government indifference, and by the increasing corruption of union leadership in conjunction with employer and Wall Street support. I (Mills) spoke to the leadership of the American unions during the 1980s about resisting the tide of American jobs shifting overseas, and about resisting the key role of Wall Street in this. The response was that Wall Street had so infiltrated the leadership of American unions via benefit funds that nothing could be done by top union leadership.

These things have been known to the American establishment, our governing class, for decades. A clear and concise explanation was given in that most establishment of American periodicals, *Foreign Affairs*.

The push into hyperglobalization since the 1990s has led to much greater levels of international economic integration. At the same time, it has produced domestic disintegration. As professional, corporate and financial elites have connected with their peers all over the globe, they have grown more distant from their compatriots at home. Today's populist backlash is a symptom of that fragmentation. (Dani Rodrik, "Globalization's Wrong Turn," *Foreign Affairs*, 98 (4), July/August, 2019, p. 33.)

A pair of authors have urged establishment figures, whom they refer to as *moderates*, to crush the populist uprising.

Moderates must avoid the impulse to borrow from the populists' illiberal playbook, even as they find a way to re-imagine the institutions that once served us well. The endless news cycle of outrage is exhausting and contributes to what some see as a "normalization" of behavior that would have been all but unthinkable only a few years ago. Yet if we have learned anything from 2016, it is that the insecurities trembling beneath the surface are not mechanical responses to any single political event or economic crisis. Rather, they have been building over decades in the face of profound social, demographic, and cultural change, which has fractured the basis for social trust. The emergence of effective populist campaigners on all sides has given voice and legitimacy to existing frustrations, while depicting the battle for the country's future as an existential choice. (Dalibor Rohac and Sophia Gaston, "The Flight 93 Temptation," *American Interest*, September 5, 2019, https://www.the-american-interest.com/2019/09/05/the-flight-93-temptation/.)

Establishment politicians bemoan the abandonment of the common people at home and promise to rectify the situation. They do not. The establishment does not act. By mid-2019, recognition of the problem had become so widespread that a major business organization declared its purpose to start considering the interests of employees and customers along with those of shareholders when its executives made decisions. That is, so-called stakeholder interests were to displace shareholder primacy in the governance of corporations. There was no immediate indication what the consequence would be, if any, of this declaration — but the declaration showed that the problem was known to the American establishment.

A large majority of the American electorate now voices deep discontent with America's governance. These are the people who have become marginalized and who are the rising numbers of the populists and progressives. In large part this is due to a group of major grievances:

I'm left out of the economy.

If I can get a job, it's not a good one and I'm exploited by my employer.

It's a two-tier justice system and I'm in the bottom tier.

I'm held in contempt, insulted, and excluded by the establishment.

I'm envious of the favoritism shown to favored groups.

I have no political say because politics is dominated by those with money to give the politicians and I don't have enough money to give it away.

America has become much more socially stratified in the past few decades. Many Americans feel left out of the advances that have been made — they can't afford them. An elite has developed. Even before the American Revolution, we had an elite of income and wealth. In the early days of our republic there were struggles between the haves and have-nots. Nonetheless, in the 1940s and 1950s these divisions lessened. Then in later decades, they again worsened. The divisions now seem to be at a very high level.

The broad dissatisfaction has depopulated the ranks of traditional liberal Democrats and traditional conservative Republicans. Liberals and conservatives have not answered the pleas of the masses. So castaways have been looking elsewhere in our political landscape for succor. Our have-littles are now living lives of quiet desperation and unfulfilled needs.

The appeal of progressivism is to people who are desperate and angry and want government to help them directly.

The appeal of populism is to people who want to find in government an affirmation of their traditional values provided by strong leadership and verities, like patriotism.

What makes a person a populist instead of a progressive is partly whom that person blames for her or his resentment. Populists blame progressives, liberals, and the swamp. Progressives blame riffraff populists, and the liberal white male establishment, especially those who are wealthy.

Both progressivism and populism provide hope to disillusioned have-littles and the disgruntled. Each is a major way in which the American political process is attempting to cope with a crisis created by its shortcomings and failures in recent decades.

The establishment in recent years has found it expedient to accommodate progressives, but has left populists out in the cold. This asymmetry is partly an indirect consequence of electoral sparring between Democrats and Republicans, and partly a direct result of the high budgetary costs and low electoral benefit of providing additional services to common people.

Most Democratic and Republican office-holders in Washington find it convenient to overburden the middle and blue-collar working class and under-provide common people with public services, while enriching themselves by supporting the agendas of Wall Street and big social activism. The two political parties differ only in partisan emphasis and patronage. Democrats construct their collective identities around the entitlement social justice theme, while Republicans focus on reducing taxation, increasing economic growth, and promising prosperity. Democrats are stronger advocates of international involvements for the United States, but establishment Republicans are also involved.

Democrats and Republicans both have embraced outsourcing as a device for turning government into a *public service business* for their own personal benefit. Public services today are not state-owned undertakings. The government hires private companies to do the job. Many contractors (outsourcers) are owned or controlled by politicians or are large corporations who return favors to politicians via campaign contributions and under-the-table kickbacks. (Steven Rosefielde and Quinn Mills, *Democracy and Its Elected Enemies,* Cambridge: Cambridge University Press, 2013.) Democrats and Republicans fight hard and spend fortunes to be elected because winning allows them to control a patronage machine that today not only provides public jobs to people but also lucrative public contracts and protection for private interests via government regulation of industry. Some politicians may believe that big government is the best vehicle for serving their constituencies, but even those that do not, understand that expanded federal spending is the ticket to their personal wealth and power.

The hallmarks of establishment rule are politically lucrative government programs, over-regulation, open immigration, and over-taxation borne by the middle class. Proponents of big social activism and big business charge handsomely for their *public services* and are lightly taxed. Transfers are provided to the poor, immigrants, entitled, and privileged at both ends of the income spectrum, paid for by the cash cow which is the common man. From the perspective of the establishment, the lower- and upper-end beneficiaries never have enough, while the middle never has too little. Democrats drive the system toward social programs (affirmative action, entitlements, and restorative justice) when they hold the reins of power; Republicans drive the system toward business deregulation, with both factions oblivious to the secular decline induced by stultifying regulation and worker labor force withdrawal (claiming disability) to join the privileged lower depths. This establishment system tends to cause economic stagnation, but it is self-perpetuating as long as stifling regulation is not pushed to extremes, and the middle class is reconciled to its plight.

The establishment denies that big government, regulation, open immigration, entitlements, and taxation are excessive, but nonetheless has adopted arcane incentive schemes, expansionary monetary and fiscal policies, and financial liberalization to try to mitigate the damage. First, it depresses the patient with barbiturates, and then tries to turbocharge it with amphetamines, claiming that both therapies are for the best, even though the middle class knows better.

The discrepancy between the common man's experience and the establishment's sunshine narrative is largely ignored by academia and the media (except for the plight of aggrieved progressives). Both academia and the media are integral parts of the system. Academic economists divert attention from the plight of the middle class by claiming that the establishment has the tools at its disposal to assure that everyone prospers, and that government beneficially employs superior administration and market competition. Democratic and Republican economists both insist that more can be done for their constituencies, ignoring the fact that ordinary people are paying the piper. They contend that sophisticated planning and management techniques mean that government programs are efficient and will remain so as programs ceaselessly expand. They contend that markets assure prosperity and over-regulation-induced economic anemia has reliable macroeconomic remedies, squabbling among themselves about the wisdom of emphasizing monetary and fiscal stimulus, supplemented by financial deregulations. Instead of spotlighting the establishment's baneful consequences, most academics limit themselves to praising the system and choosing partisan sides. The media drums home the message.

The results of the establishment system, however, are there for all to see. Despite trillions spent on eradicating poverty, the poverty rate has changed little in 50 years. Despite the current opioid crisis, and after hundreds of billions spent on the war against drugs, the establishment can only report as positive that it is legalizing pot. Despite a 20 trillion dollar federal debt and a quintupling of the money supply after 2010, America's economy is barely able to grow at half its historical rate. Despite countless promises, the middle class is drifting toward poverty. The establishment system is failing the middle class and spawning social discord, but politicians, the media, and academics respond by denying this. It is an exercise in hypocrisy.

The stealthy advance of the establishment's system galls populists. It interests progressives who want to gain more for themselves from the establishment's system. Democrats are recognizing this by proposing more and more redistribution, but the experience of the last few decades reveals that the sum and substance of their efforts is widening the gulf between the rich and the common people.

It is useful to note that what we have described in detail as occurring in America is also occurring in similar fashion abroad. For example, the political dynamic in France mimics the United States. Populist working and rural people are furious at the establishment whether or not it is right or left in the old ideological leanings (as in France) or in the traditional partisan alignments (as in the United States). The demonstrations of the so-called *yellow vests* in France are an expression of resentment and rage by working people at the establishment and rising inequality. The protests have been organized primarily on social media. With minor concessions to the demonstrators, the French establishment seems to have held on to its position at the moment, which has also happened in the United States thus far, despite the victory of presidential candidates in both the United States and France who gave voice to populist anger.

The life of the middle class worsens. The working class is disappearing into a general proletariat. The core political reason for this is that the Republicans support business exploitation of the middle class and working class while the Democrats seek to coax the middle and working class into a left-leaning, government-dependent underclass. The middle and working class is faced with exploitation and marginalization. This is the root cause of the populist attraction.

In this situation, both political parties make empty promises to improve the lot of common people. Neither are sincere. The Democrats under progressive influence prefer a lumpen proletariat (a have-little working class). Democrats promise to strengthen the middle and working class, but continually undermine it instead.

Republicans promise benefits to the middle and working class but are committed to exploiting them on behalf of much of the business community. Republicans support big business while misleadingly promising to support competitive middle-class small and moderate-sized business. The economy they support is dominated by giant businesses and permits intensive exploitation of employees and consumers.

CHAPTER TWELVE

THE STRUGGLE FOR THE VOTES OF A CHANGING ELECTORATE

The majority of the American electorate is now anti-establishment. Most are strongly so. They are the voters who will support populism or progressivism. There is a contest among the populists and progressives for the allegiance of these voters. The winner will likely control American politics for decades. What are the characteristics of these voters?

There is continual discussion of the changing character of the American electorate. Most of it centers on the numbers of people in various ethnic groups. The general outlines are well-known. The white population is growing slowly, and the non-white population is growing rapidly, due to immigration and higher birth rates. However, the picture is fuzzier than it seems because it is unclear who is white and non-white. Hispanics are generally counted as non-white, but many, if not most, Hispanics are white. They are descendants of Spanish, Portuguese, Italian, and German immigrants to South America. If an adjustment is made for this, then the white population is larger than ordinarily said. Nonetheless, the non-white population, however defined, is growing more rapidly than the white. The non-white is still smaller than the white population, but this must reverse if the trend persists.

The impact of these demographic changes on politics is dramatic. The Democrats have focused their attention on non-whites and

Hispanics for decades. As they have shifted their orientation to these ethnic groups, they have lost interest in common white people. This is less true of the liberal element of the Democratic Party than it is of the progressive element. Progressives focus almost exclusively on non-whites and Hispanics, and ignore the blue-collar working class because it is mostly white.

Nonetheless, there is a substantial white membership of the progressive movement including, especially, its leadership. For example, the Democratic presidential hopefuls who are the leading progressives are both white (Senators Warren and Sanders).

While almost all discussion is about changes in the size of various demographic groups, numbers are not the only aspect of change in the electorate that matter — perhaps not even the most important. The attitudinal and skill composition of the electorate is also changing significantly and these things have a big impact on our politics. They affect how politicians appeal to the electorate and how the electorate responds. These things contribute to the increasing radicalization of our politics. They contribute directly to the shift toward progressivism and aggravate the plight of common people.

The most recent generations glued to their smartphones are wonders to their elders. They are experts at computer games, Rubik's cubes, and internet shopping. They are probably best skilled to operate the controls of drones or fighter planes. They are weak at interpersonal skills — as they themselves acknowledge continually on social media. They have limited analytical skills and are especially weak at critical thinking. They confuse technical competence with analytical skills, critical thinking, and emotional maturity. They know little history, even that of their own lifetimes. Progressive leaders tell them that all that happened before is a story of centuries of exploitation and dishonesty. Without some knowledge of how previous generations of humans dealt with issues of war and peace, of stability and revolution, younger people are ripe for repeating age-old human errors.

Many populists — no one knows the proportion — are older persons who remember a better time and wish to recapture it. Many progressives — no one knows the proportion — are younger persons who are hopeful for a better world. The populists are skeptical of the hopes of the younger people because they were themselves once young and hopeful and have been disappointed. They fear that the same disappointments await younger people. The progressives lament that the older people appear to have lost hope and vision.

The loss of so many of the young is perhaps the greatest failure of populists and conservatives. Strong efforts are now being made by conservatives to recoup the loss — particularly by an organization of college-age people led by Charlie Kirk, called Turning Point USA.

A Passing Generation

There have been two very important generations in the past 100 years of American political life. One is the generation called upon to fight World War II. The other is their children — the so-called *baby boom* generation.

Because of their victory in World War II, the generation which fought it has been called the *Greatest Generation*. It accomplished a great deal.

The parents of the Greatest Generation were not its equal. One of their most serious shortcomings was its wishful thinking — it preferred to ignore growing dangers in the world. The fighting that developed into World War II had been underway in Asia for four years and in Europe for more than two years when America was forced into the war. For all those years of conflict abroad, most Americans chose to believe that we could stay out of the war and need not prepare seriously for it. They were isolationists. Hence, the attack on Pearl Harbor was a surprise to Americans. Many people believed that if America simply acted as if the world were much safer than it was, it would become so. Today's progressives are prone to this fallacy.

As the baby boom generation matured and began to take power in America, as CEOs of our large corporations and governors, Senators, and even President, I (Mills) joined with many others in thinking about what their grasp of leadership would mean for us all. I (Mills) wrote a book entitled *Not Like Our Parents* (D. Quinn Mills, *Not Like Our*

Parents: How The Baby Boom Generation Is Changing America, New York: William Morrow, 1987), describing a baby boom generation that was determined from a young age to forge a course in life for itself that was very different from that of its parents. It seemed to have great strengths — strengths that would be equal to its opportunities.

It is now 30 years since I published the book about the baby boom generation. The book was very positive. The first baby boomers were then moving into top positions in American business, education, and government. The first baby boomer president — Bill Clinton — would take office in 1992. The baby boomers seemed to have great promise.

The boomers were the children of the Greatest Generation that survived the Great Depression and won World War II. How did their children fare?

Never before was a generation so pampered. It received love, care, resources, and a good example from its parents. How did it use its advantages?

The Greatest Generation handed over the world in good shape with America's role in it never more significant. The United States in 1990 was the sole superpower. The USSR had collapsed a year previously.

The boomers were determined to create a world more to their liking, and in doing so, they dismantled the world their parents had made and threw it all out — the good with the bad, the baby with the bathwater.

Many baby boomers, strongly influenced by Vietnam War radicalism, took over the leadership of America in the 1990s. Bill Clinton was the first baby boomer President of the United States, followed by two others thereafter. George W. Bush and Barack Obama are clearly baby boomers. Donald Trump is on the line between baby boomers and the Great Generation that preceded them. It is fair to say that we have had four baby boomer presidents.

Baby boomers are numerous and, since the 1990s, have dominated all aspects of American society. Their promise as young people was enormous. Their record as leaders has been lackluster.

Among older figures who worked with baby boomer and previous presidents, the judgment is common that the baby boomer presidents are all empty suits. None has had the sort of character-building experience that most presidents had had before. Truman served in combat during World War I. Eisenhower commanded Allied forces in Europe during World War II. John F. Kennedy fought in World War II; Nixon served in World War II; Reagan served in World War II but did not see combat. However, he fought bitter battles against the Communists when he was President of the Screen Actors Guild. George H.W. Bush fought in World War II. There are no exceptions to the seasoning of American presidents through military service until the ascension of the baby boomers. After that, without exception, American presidents have found a way to avoid combat service (though George W. Bush argues that this is not so).

All four of our baby boomer presidents avoided real military service. In elections, the country seems to have preferred candidates who avoided military service. This is presumably one of the many overhangs of the unpopular Vietnam War.

We thought that the Vietnam War was an exception, an outlier, a black swan. We thought that when it ended, the country would revert to the attitudes and behaviors of the 1950s and early 1960s. We thought the turmoil and anti-establishment attitudes of the war years would dissipate.

They did not. The Vietnam War resuscitated the unrest of the Depression years and it has grown slowly and steadily ever since. A letter to the *New York Times* in 1991 said, "Having grown up in the 1960s, I never met a protest I didn't like…. It seemed such an American thing to do." (Jacques Barzun, *From Dawn to Decadence*, New York: Harper Collins, 2000, p. 783.) The result is the anti-establishment feelings of today and the contest between populist and progressive to express and embody the dissatisfaction of the masses.

A result is that the four baby boomer presidents have made a mess of the presidency.

To listen to the children of the baby boomers, their parents are perhaps the worst generation we have had. The baby boomers wasted government entitlement programs so that their children believe they cannot count on programs such as Social Security and Medicare. These children of baby boomers are increasingly demanding that baby boomers retire in order to make job and promotion opportunities available to them. They try to humiliate their parents by calling them *Mr. Boomer* and *Mrs. Boomer*. The children of the Greatest Generation, that is, the boomers, are being cast aside by what may soon be labeled the *Clueless Generation*.

Baby boomers received none of their parents' virtues, but all of their vices. They chose to make their parents' vices that they inherited seem like virtues. They made virtues of adultery, drug use, and greed, and belittled patriotism.

World War II shaped the Greatest Generation. The Vietnam War made baby boomers suspicious, belligerent, arrogant, and self-righteous.

Boomers are a very self-conscious generation. From adolescence, they defined themselves as different from their parents. They criticized their parents and sought to be different. Boomers set out to carve a separate identity for themselves and transform the world. Today many young people are seeking to forge their own iconoclastic course.

What are their prospects?

Victims of the Baby Boomers

While boomers greatly exceeded their parents in living standards, boomers' children are likely to be the first generation of Americans to do less well economically than their parents.

Boomers have let their own health deteriorate, and that of their children. Life expectancy has declined for four consecutive years. Americans now have the highest obesity rates of any nation in history. This is surprising since a vast amount of attention, research, and experimentation has been devoted by boomers to personal fitness and exercise. Many boomers are among the fittest and healthiest persons ever to have lived. Marathons are host to tens of thousands of runners. Extreme sports are popular. Yet, most Americans have followed a different course, and personal fitness is at its lowest in our history. Most American young people are not fit for military service. The grandchildren of the Greatest Generation are not able to follow in their parents' footsteps to help preserve our country militarily should the need arise. Boomers have left their children and grandchildren with limited incomes, low savings, and lots of debt. What they have gathered, they have spent on themselves.

In an assessment that populists today would surely support, Will and Ariel Durant wrote, "Caught in the relaxing interval between one moral code and the next [should there be one], an unmoored generation surrenders itself to luxury, disruption and a reckless disorder of family and morals." (Will and Ariel Durant, *The Lessons of History*, NY: Simon and Schuster, 1968, p. 93.)

Seldom has more promise been so thoroughly wasted.

What went wrong? What caused the transition from the patriotism of World War II to the cynicism of today? At its foundation was the spoiled upbringing of the baby boomers. The political failures of the World War II generation (the Greatest Generation) were also crucial.

Baby boomers are not entirely to blame. It was the Greatest Generation that gave us the Vietnam War, a disaster so significant that it has affected American political attitudes until today. In 1960, before the war, Americans had an 80 percent favorable rating of our federal government and by the same margin trusted our national leaders. Today, those ratings are close to 10 percent.

John F. Kennedy took us into the Vietnam War. He did it for geopolitical reasons. He put only our toes into the hot water. He could have gotten us out of the conflict, and intended to, but was killed before he could do so.

Lyndon Johnson made a mess of it. As baby boomer men came of age, they were packed off to Vietnam to die in a war which was brutal but unsuccessful. This radicalized the intellectual elite for coming decades, combining old leftism with new draft resistance. The hypocrisy of the federal government was evident, as was its indecision and ineptitude — it lost the war and our sacrifices seemed in vain. Many boomers did not trust government, as a result, and retreated into selfishness in all aspects of life, where many still seem to be.

The foundations of the radicalization of American politics discussed above can be seen as having their roots in the leadership of the American economy and society by boomers — that is, in having a generational basis. Boomers can be charged with letting good jobs disappear and picking their children's pockets. They allowed housing costs to rise so that their offspring cannot purchase homes and cannot therefore build up equity and net worth for retirement. This has kept savings rates so low that savings cannot be built up for investments, college costs, and home ownership. In effect, boomers spent everything (government and private debt have been built up) on themselves, bequeathing the debt baby to their descendants.

Boomers also bear responsibility for fostering immoderate progressive activism. Their counter-cultural proclivities infected the educational system and are encouraging the post-boomer generation to misperceive reality and favor confrontation over social harmony.

In the end, a poorly educated, largely non-attentive but opinionated electorate is easy prey to demagogues.

PART V

"FOR GOD'S SAKE, DON'T TRY TO IMPROVE THEIR MINDS!"

American politics is increasingly complex. Voters are supposed to get much of the information to base their voting behavior from the mass media. Mass media has evolved from primarily newspapers to television and periodicals and now to social media. How well is it doing its job?

CHAPTER THIRTEEN

THE ROLE OF MASS MEDIA

Years ago, I (Mills) was asked at a large conference in New York City to comment on the role of mass media in American public life. I mentioned how important the media is to our political system. I praised it for informing and educating the people. Today, I am ashamed of those remarks, because they indicate how divorced I was from what was even then occurring in American public life.

Today the media has only one thing of importance — access to large numbers of people. This is more and more important because a variety of factors have fragmented the American electorate, making it is very difficult for most politicians to obtain a large audience. Political rallies generally attract very few people. The exceptions are the rallies of a few major politicians who, for a while, are celebrities themselves. Celebrities attract large audiences, as do rock concerts and professional sports games.

In an environment where audiences are hard to obtain, media access is very valuable. The American media uses that access for its own purposes, and it denies that access to others. People think of the media as a public service — it ought to be, but is not. At its best, America's media expresses the opinions of private groups of owners; at its worst, it is the propaganda outlet for a political party or even an administration. What the media says in its overwhelming support of the left in American politics upsets many people. What is equally important is what it ignores and keeps out of the public discussion.

In recent years, with the emergence of populism and progressivism, the media has degenerated greatly. It no longer performs its necessary role in our democracy. The big problem with the American media is its failure to live up to the great responsibility that the American political system places on it. It has a duty to provide accurate information and education about public issues. Today's American media is a miserable failure at both. It is shallow in the information it provides, often errone-ous, and it is distinctly partisan rather than educational.

In the best of American political novels, Robert Penn Warren's *All The King's Men* (Bantam, 1959), Willie Stark, a young and idealistic candidate for public office gives honest and informative speeches to audiences in rural Louisiana. Slowly his audiences dwindle. A discour-aged Willie asks a reporter who has been covering his campaign, Jack Burden, what is wrong. Burden replies, "Make 'em laugh! Make 'em cry! But for God's sake don't try to improve their minds!"

Entering politics wholeheartedly, the American media has taken to heart Jack's advice. It makes no effort to improve the minds of its audi-ence. Yet it lacks the justification that Willie Stark had for following Jack's advice. Willie was looking for votes. The American media is only looking for an audience. The American media wraps itself in a sup-posed professionalism of journalism, but perverts it generally for finan-cial gain. Newspapers have done this for centuries. TV news is now a profit center for networks where it used to be a public service. As such, it has degraded its role. It no longer plays the critical role it is supposed to play in our democracy. It whines continually about threats to our democracy, and ignores its own major role as a threat.

If media outlets or politicians themselves should try to educate American voters about key issues, the effort would be much more dif-ficult today than a few decades ago. This is because the media have now so filled the minds of voters with disinformation that a reporter or a commentator or a politician trying to improve the minds of voters would not only have to give them more information, it would also have to deprogram them of all the disinformation they have acquired and believe to be true. When we have written previous books, we have had to begin by saying to our readers, "In order to understand what we have to share with you, you must first try to jettison all the disinformation you have picked up from the media. That will take us a while."

The way the media interacts with the progressive leadership was on display October 27, 2019 when President Trump went on TV to announce the success of an American special forces operation in Syria that eliminated the top leadership of ISIS. Trump claimed partial credit for the operation in a speech to the American people and a press conference following. CNN carried almost the full 45 minutes of Trump's appearance. The operation was a strong success for the President. In its immediate aftermath, it appeared that CNN program managers and on-camera reporters had no idea how to spin the news against the President. They brought onto camera and interviewed Republican lawmakers who praised the President. CNN was waiting for direction as to how to formulate an anti-Trump spin — the ordinary procedure of partisan politics in the United States today. Presumably, because these things are almost never public, the top leadership of the Democratic Party — very likely former President Obama and his close entourage — and its intellectual leadership at the *New York Times* and the *Washington Post* were at that time formulating a pro-progressive spin. They would soon publicize it. CNN and other pro-progressive media outlets picked it up. When Trump saw it, he labeled it "fake news."

Within a short time, the progressive response was made. The *Washington Post* had changed its characterization of the leader of ISIS who had been killed from a terrorist to "an austere, religious scholar." The implication seemed to be that the President should not have approved killing him. Interviewees on CNN were criticizing Trump for how he had handled his announcement, including for taking questions from the press, and for needlessly provoking Islamic radicals by killing a "scholarly" terrorist leader.

It is common in the news business for a publisher or producer to assure their audience that editorials are separated from news. However, this is no assurance at all. In effect, it says, "We're going to propagandize you, even mislead you, about politics, but you should trust us about everything else." This cannot be assuring.

Most news is manufactured by the media itself — interviews, reports, analyses, commentary, surveys, speculation. There is little fact in all this *news*.

Reporters and most commentators comment freely on what they do not understand in any depth.

This is how the American system now operates. Whether a person admires or condemns it depends in large part on what they think of how our system should operate — should the party out of power always criticize the actions of the party in power or should there be some evidence of support when the national interest is involved?

Americans choose their media outlets based on their political leanings. It is common for leftists to shun media thought to be conservative or populist in orientation. Rightists do the same thing. They shun liberal and progressive media outlets. Media outlets choose their political orientation and stick with it. This behavior by outlets and audiences increase the divide in understanding between left and right in our country. There is a conservative mass media in America and there is a liberal/progressive mass media. There is a much smaller populist mass media confined almost exclusively to the internet.

Perhaps the reason that the media is looking for an audience today takes a side in our political wars is that the political orientation of people is so firmly fixed. We have seen in an earlier chapter that most Americans today choose a particular political orientation and do not change it. In fact, most rule out any information or opinion that might shake their orientation. So if a media business (and they are all businesses) is seeking a reliable audience, it is likely to adopt a particular orientation which will attract and hold people who are of that orientation. A network may adopt only liberal positions and information; another network may adopt only progressive news and positions. Fewer networks may adopt conservative news and positions; and very few currently adopt populist news and positions.

So few networks adopt populist positions when there are in fact tens of millions of populist voters in America that it is obvious that another force is at work, overcoming the commercial incentive for business media to appeal directly to populists. That force is rooted in the progressive-leaning colleges and universities training the professionals who become anchors, reporters, and commentators in the media. Media companies find it much easier to staff progressive outlets, and find it difficult to keep an outlet conservative or populist if it starts that way. The professional staff move it leftward.

There is an exception to the focus of progressive media outlets on progressive topics and the exclusion of conservative and populist topics. That is the large amount of coverage given President Trump on all media for his populist messages. The populist media is almost always favorable to Trump; the conservative media is generally negative but moderate in tone. The liberal media is invariably negative to Trump but moderate in tone. The progressive media is always negative and hysterical in tone. So while Trump is covered continually in the progressive media, for example, the coverage is always with a negative spin — and the shriller the negative spin, the more popular it seems to be with progressive audiences. Leftist media seem oblivious to the consequences of their unceasing attacks on the President. Trump is not just a politician, he is the President of the United States. He cannot be excoriated daily without damaging the presidency and the nation. Indeed that is what is occurring. The United States becomes collateral damage in the war waged by the media on the President. It could not be otherwise.

The American mass news media is a for-profit commercial activity, with strong partisan affiliations, propagandizing to secure a reliable audience. It contributes to the radicalization of American politics, primarily in support of progressive causes.

There seem to be a few anchors, reporters, and commentators who have valuable insights about American politics, society and our economy. It is too bad that they cannot be fully objective in their comments, but instead have to work for one or another network, newspaper, magazine, or internet outlet which is devoted to one of the political orientations — that is, they can only express opinions that are acceptable to progressives, or liberals, or conservatives, or populists. They are constrained in their reporting by the political orientation of their employer.

Moreover, many people in our country get morally indignant at reports they hear or read in the media. They express their indignation strongly.

When the reports are wrong — by accident or intentionally — and other people know they are wrong, then the indignation appears ridiculous and the people who express the opinions look like fools.

An extreme and very common case of this arises when a person develops very strong opinions about a public figure and expresses them.

"Do you know personally that person whom you are denouncing?" the speaker might be asked.

"Oh, no. I would never want to meet him!"

"So your strong opinion is based solely on media reports?"

"Yes."

"Do you trust the media like that in other things?"

"No."

"Then what is this about?"

The answer is that there is no basis for such a strong opinion and expressing it makes the speaker seem a fool. This happens all the time now in the United States.

Populists have felt from the beginning of the current political cycle in 2015 that the media have been openly hostile. Trump has complained about it often and coined the term *fake news* to characterize the situation. Somewhat dispassionate analyses by opposing institutions, including Harvard's Kennedy School of Government, confirm that media mentions of the Trump Administration are overwhelmingly negative. From the populist perspective, two other of the Nazi/Communist rules of political engagement are being confirmed as used by the enemies of populism — namely that lies repeated over and over gain credence even if they are refuted. The bigger the lie, the more likely it is to be believed — for example, that populism is a current-day form of Nazism, or populist leadership is racist.

Because of concerns about media bias, populist political leaders, particularly President Trump, have been urged since before his election to create a populist-leaning network. Trump has spoken of creating such a network repeatedly, right up to the present day, but no decisive steps have been taken. From the earliest day of his campaign, Trump has complained about the news coverage and continues to do so. Why has there been no action? Perhaps it is hard to do; perhaps the effort is crowded out by other concerns. Perhaps populists continue to hope that media coverage will become more balanced, although there is no indication that that is happening. The failure to establish a more favorably inclined network and to build an audience for it must be accounted one of the most serious shortcomings of the Trump Administration and its supporters. The consequence is that populists will go through the 2020 election cycle at a continuing disadvantage in the media.

The generality of inaccurate news and commentary on the media is now reinforcing the divisions in the American society. The Harvard/Harris poll shows that 84 percent of US voters do not know which media outlet to believe. In this situation they pick the one with which they have an affinity of thought or identity and accept what it says uncritically. This is one of the ways in which propaganda-like news outlets become dominant with certain audiences.

Reinforcing the low reliability of the media is the declining knowledge of the American population. The proportion of our population with longer years of schools completed and with higher credentials than in the past (high school diplomas, for example) is rising. However, the actual performance of these people is falling. Many high school graduates are now functionally illiterate. Young people accepted into college programs have serious learning deficiencies and schools have to provide remedial education for many. Facing this situation, many professors teach watered-down courses. Half-truths are intentionally put forward which support specific political positions. The result is that we have a poorly educated generation that believes it is fully educated and knows the truth about many things. It is in fact a generation skilled only in technological skills and is naive politically, led by media sensationalism and demagoguery.

It is disheartening that the media is mostly psychobabble.

Lester C. Thurow was for several years the primary academic spokesperson of the liberals in American politics. He was one of the leaders in President Lyndon Johnson's creation of the national anti-poverty program. I (Mills) worked with him in the early days of the Office of Economic Opportunity (OEO), headed by Sargent Shriver, John and Bobby Kennedy's brother-in-law. Les was at the White House and I was in the OEO. Later Les was dean of the Sloan School of Management school at MIT. He was sometimes wrong but always honest. He would listen to other points of view and when persuaded, would change his views. The foremost of his successors — two were required to cover his breadth — is almost always wrong and never honest. That is made possible by the steady decline of the knowledge and sophistication of the American public.

In early October 2019, President Trump announced the withdrawal of the small number of remaining US troops in northeast Syria to permit a Turkish incursion into the region. The media made no attempt to understand what the President was doing and gave only the briefest mention of his general explanation. Instead, it immediately ran establishment attacks on the President's action opposing force reductions in the region, and attacks from the Democrats opposed to anything Trump did. The numerous thoughtful reasons that could have been given for the President's action were never mentioned in the media. There were, of course, strong considerations against it. An informed public and an informed Congress that gets its news firsthand, and secondhand (via communications from constituents who are themselves informed by the media), could have made an knowledgeable decision to support or not the President's policy. This was not possible due to the simple-minded, profit-oriented posture of the American media.

In the United States in various localities, there are public interest institutions that invite speakers to public forums to discuss public issues. In principle, this is a good thing. It has great potential, and in our past — especially in the period preceding the Civil War when Lincoln toured the north discussing the issues of the day — these institutions have done great service. Today, the major speakers at these institutions are media celebrities (anchors, reporters, and commentators) and their presentations are as superficial as the news reporting they do for their employers, the networks. The result is programs of little informational value. Since most media celebrities are identified with a particular political orientation (progressive, liberal, or conservative, and a few populist, Republican or Democrat) the presentations are generally highly partisan. There is nothing more than perverse entertainment value in most of these programs. The failure of the media to perform a useful public service spills over into what used to be very valuable public information outlets.

What does the American media do well? It spins narratives that support one political agenda or another. It sensationalizes insignificant matters for political advantage. It investigates the background and pretenses of political candidates — always exposing the candidates of the other side. These things are useful, but very limited in value. They make a small soap opera contribution to the national political welfare. That's about it.

Social Media Drives Emotionalism

Social media now plays a significant role in American politics. It introduces a highly emotional and potentially mob-like element into political discussion. It de-rationalizes and radicalizes politics. The disinformation (fake news) disseminated by the mass media is compounded by the disinformation spread by populists and progressives on social media and plays a significant role in elections.

As social media increases mob-like behavior on the extremes of our political spectrum, the Mitterand Rule ensures that ambitious politicians will grasp either side in pursuit of their own careers. Thus, social media drives extremism in two ways: by circulating news bulletins which pander to either extreme of the political spectrum; and by fostering mob psychology.

CHAPTER FOURTEEN

THE CRISIS OF THE ESTABLISHMENT

It is possible to view populism, in particular, as a revolt of common people against unfair economic treatment. Populism is more this sort of revolt of the overburdened than progressivism because progressivism has leadership from the elite, while populism does not. The absence of effective populist considerable leadership is one of its greatest limitations.

If we view populism from the perspective of a revolt of the have-littles against the establishment, then history gives it a slim chance of success. History is full of grassroots revolt of the overburdened rabble against the rich, and almost always they end in tragedy for the weak. As a single example, in 1196, when Richard the Lionheart was King of England, there was an uprising of the poor in London over unfair taxation. The leader of the revolt, the 2nd Earl of Salisbury, was executed brutally and the revolt was suppressed. The few revolts that succeed are almost always of the progressive type which are led by members of the elite. Examples are the French, Russian, and Chinese revolutions. American populism at this point does not have elite leadership. Trump's wealth does not make him a member of the elite — at best, he is an outlier; at worst, he is a reject. If history is any guide, the revolt of American populism against the establishment will fail. The effort to remove Trump by impeachment can be viewed from this perspective as the suppression of a revolt of the ordinary people by the establishment. It may be objected that not all the overburdened have joined the populist revolt in America. This is true, but it was equally true of populist revolts in the past.

Both populism and progressivism are reactions against the establishment governing America. What is this establishment?

The *establishment* is a set of people who hold significant positions in government or business and who largely know each other and abide by certain conventions of behavior. When I (Mills) first entered a position in Washington as a young man, I was cautioned by a friend about how not to personalize political and policy differences and refrain from publicly criticizing establishment members. Others have published accounts of similar introductions to the American establishment.

The establishment, in the early 1960s when I (Mills) entered its lower level, was driven in part by greed for personal advancement and wealth and in part by patriotism — a follow-on from World War II and the Korean War. It was possible in those days to appeal to the patriotism of most Americans to accomplish a public purpose. There was then almost no rejection by Americans of an appeal to patriotism.

Today, the establishment is driven by greed, with a pretense of patriotism. An appeal to patriotism is met positively by only a few members of the establishment and is rejected by many. This is not true of all Washington people, but it is true of many of them. Most politicians are careerists of the Mitterand type — indifferent to the causes they represent and interested primarily in their own advancement.

Americans, sensing this, have become wary of their government.

The establishment can be confused with *politicrats* (garden variety venal politicians using the state for personal enrichment). However, America's establishment is about more than personal enrichment. The establishment has a consensus policy agenda. Establishment persons operate within an agreed framework, and may be considered an informal conspiracy.

The American establishment (politicians and allies) is composed of liberal Democrats and conservative Republicans, many of whom are perplexed by the rapid radicalization of America's politics. Liberal and conservative members sense the danger and fear losing their grip on power.

Establishment members come from various walks of American life, not just politics and government. Some are businessmen, academics, non-governmental organization (NGOs) members, lawyers, and some labor representatives. They are organization leaders, many of whom know each other. Many serve on the same boards and committees, and thereby interlock. They are aware of each other and the conventions binding them together.

When I (Mills) arrived at the Harvard Business School in the mid-1970s, a report had just been issued identifying the Dean of the Harvard Business School as the largest single interlock among American corporations. He served on multiple boards and linked the major firms via his membership on their boards. I recall mentioning this to a friend on the faculty of another school who was not part of the establishment. He responded immediately, "How embarrassing for you!" He thought of the interlocking of boards as a form of corruption and scandalous. Members of the establishment did not think of it that way.

Outsiders see much of the interlocking, favorable dealing, and traded favors as corrupt. For the most part it is not illegal since the Supreme Court of the United States refuses to see illegal corruption in government and business except when it takes the most simple, direct and naive form of a specific *this for that* — a direct *quid pro quo*. No one who is sophisticated does anything so direct. One of the most important lessons in business school is that payment does not have to be simultaneous with performance. That is, if a public official does something to benefit me, I can wait for a long time before paying him or her via a job, or a contract, or just a financial award. Doing this requires a bit of trust — the person performing the service has to trust that the recipient will actually pay in the future when there is no written contract or way to make the recipient pay. Nonetheless, meeting in an honorable fashion one's obligation under a corrupt agreement is an important convention of the establishment. Thus to a naive outsider, or to the Supreme Court, there will be no evidence of corruption.

These agreed frameworks and conventions of how things can be done (like divorcing payment from performance so there are no bribes) are very powerful factors in shaping how the establishment works and how it governs.

Many ordinary Americans who are not burdened by the myopia of the Supreme Court's vision are aware of the establishment's massive corruption.

The Washington establishment is a key part of the national establishment. It is a small incestuous group. However, it is not tightly closed. It is open to new members who arrive by a variety of means including, especially, employment with major law firms, clerking in the federal courts, serving as aides in Congress, or election to Congress. To work one's way into the establishment is a major career objective of many Americans.

The Washington establishment is composed primarily of attorneys or people who have served as attorneys. Among this group are many interlocks. For example, the person who wrote the report of the Starr team, which found that Vincent Foster had committed suicide and thereby exonerated the Clintons from widespread suspicion that they had ordered Foster's murder, was Bret Kavanaugh. In doing this, Kavanaugh had done a great service to the Clintons, the Clinton Administration and the Democratic Party. Two decades later, a Republican administration nominated Kavanaugh to the Supreme Court and the Democrats attacked him personally and harshly. They were trying to block the confirmation of his appointment to the Court. The episode of the Kavanaugh appointment, like so many things in Washington, was played out to a significant degree among people who had known each other for decades and who had been on different political sides of many issues. As vicious as the Democrat attacks were on Kavanaugh, they still operated within the conventions (standards) of the establishment.

There is more. The person who drafted the report of the Starr team to the House of Representatives that suggested impeachment of President Clinton was Bret Kavanaugh. He had done a great favor for President Clinton and a great disservice. It is possible to argue that he was an honest person following the facts where they led him. It is also possible to argue that he was a careerist trying to advance up the career ladder in Washington by currying favor first with one side and then another.

There are many, many such personalities involved in American government and politics, though very few of them reach the high level of appointment and confirmation to a seat on the Supreme Court.

The establishment has ranks. At the top are people who by virtue of their office or of their contacts are decision-makers. Then there are many who are players — who have some influence in decisions that are made but do not have the authority or power to make decisions. There are also those who personally have minor or peripheral roles in the establishment.

The establishment runs the United States. Whatever the political orientation of its members, they almost all have a *status quo* bent. Their situation is comfortable and they are not anxious to see it altered, whatever else they might tell the media and their constituents.

The social and economic system that the establishment leads generates inequality. Conservatives believe this is necessary and appropriate. Liberals challenge aspects of the system. Nonetheless, both conservatives and liberals in the establishment are for the most part deeply committed to the *status quo*.

Populists and progressives would like to see major, even revolutionary, changes in the system. Over the centuries, the American establishment has turned back numerous challenges to the basic features of American society and government. There was a major challenge at the end of the 19th century from farmers and workers when William Jennings Bryan gave his "cross of gold" speech. Bryan's challenge was turned back.

There was a major challenge at the time of the Great Depression of the 1930s. A challenge from the far left, including the Communist Party USA, was conducted for more than a decade and was turned back by the Democratic Party (although at the time, and still to a degree today, conservatives believed that Franklin Roosevelt's New Deal was in fact a defeat of the American establishment).

The establishment did not expect the Republican Party to nominate a populist candidate for President in 2016. It expected even less the victory of that candidate. The result was that the Republican establishment would like to see Trump out and Pence (a conservative, not a populist, though he has been very loyal to Trump) in. For the populists there is always the danger that the Republican establishment will seize an opportunity to join with the Democrats to drive Trump out of office. Since before his inauguration, there has been a campaign to force Trump out. From the first, it has appeared as a much more sophisticated activity than simply a leftist media frenzy as portrayed in the conservative media. It sometimes has the appearance of a joint establishment (Republican and Democratic) second effort to get rid of the populist movement — the first effort was to stop Trump's nomination; the recent one has been to throw him out of the White House. The establishment fears that they might not win at the ballot box against the populists, especially if progressives splinter from the Democratic Party, so they seek success in the Washington arena, where they might win.

America's establishment today is committed to certain directions in public policy. It is committed first to maintaining its influence and privileges. With the exception of most progressives, it is also committed to maintaining America's effort to dominate the world order. Whenever a progressive politician (like Tulsi Gabbard) calls for an end to our lengthy wars and other military presence anywhere in the world, the establishment rises in immediate opposition. There are several reasons for this. Elements of the establishment like Wall Street are strong supporters of the Western world order abroad, including free trade, the rule of law, and human rights. Others are close allies of the military-industrial establishment in America and prosper from military spending.

The efforts of progressives to reduce America's role in military conflict in the world are always resisted quickly and vigorously by the establishment.

The establishment is being pulled away from its moorings — Republicans toward anti-Wall Street populism and Democrats toward anti-liberal progressivism. This leaves Republican conservatives and Democrat liberals bewildered and increasingly ineffective in national politics.

The Republican establishment at the state and local level is being dissolved even as it gains ground in offices against the Democrats. The companies and the churches no longer direct it as electoral power shifts toward the populists. At the non-federal level, the establishment is without direction and will soon lose unity of vision and action.

The establishment has lost its ability to control the selection process for presidential candidates from the two parties.

The enhanced role of primaries in the nomination process of each of the major political parties is leading to a splintering and radicalization of politics generally. As has been repeatedly pointed out by commentators in recent decades, the most likely voters in primaries are the zealots of each party — the populists among the Republicans and the progressives among the Democrats. Conservatives and liberals hold their views strongly, but do not vote proportionately as strongly as do progressives. The mass of voters in each party and among independents (independents alone make up about one-third of the national electorate) vote in much smaller numbers in the primaries. Since the primaries are increasingly important in choosing the presidential candidates of each party, the more radical elements in each have gained considerable control of the nomination process. A candidate of the Democratic Party who expresses middle-of-the-road viewpoints because he or she believes most voters in a general election prefer those viewpoints will not get the nod in the primaries and will not therefore be a candidate in the general election. It follows that a major characteristic of American politics is that a presidential candidate for the Democratic Party tends to move her or his positions toward the middle as the general election approaches, hoping to gain the votes of a mass of potential voters who are not staunch progressives. Trump may do the same, but for a different reason. He is the populists' only option.

Until 2020, the Democratic establishment kept an effective control on the nomination process despite primaries that pushed the party to the left. The Republican establishment had lost control of the nomination process long before. In 2016, the Democrats turned aside a progressive challenger, Senator Bernie Sanders, in favor of a liberal candidate, former Senator Hillary Clinton, while the Republicans were unable to avoid having to nominate a populist candidate despite the unhappiness of the Party's establishment.

What occasioned this result? The Democrats had a process by which public office-holders from the Democratic Party were voting delegates to their presidential nominating convention *ex officio* (that is, by virtue of their offices). They were called *super-delegates* and comprised about 20 percent of the voting delegates. Overwhelmingly, in 2016, the super-delegates supported the nomination of Hillary Clinton for president and their weight in the balance of delegates earned by the candidates in the primary elections made certain that the nomination would go to her — and it did.

The Republicans had no super-delegates. Trump won enough delegates in the primaries to be nominated for president and was so nominated.

Sander's backers harshly criticized the Democratic Party for their allegedly anti-democratic use of super-delegates. Even the terrible Republicans did not have them. So for 2020, the Democratic National Committee changed its rules for the nomination process. It removed super-delegates from the nomination process at the convention. Consequently, if a candidate won a majority of delegates in the primaries, she or he could be nominated by their votes at the convention.

However, this reform, as it was said to be, was limited to the first ballot at the Democratic National Convention to be held in mid-July, 2020. On the second ballot and thereafter, super-delegates would be again introduced into the nomination balloting. Thus, if there was no winner of the nomination on the first ballot, then the nominee of the Party would have to be chosen on a subsequent ballot with super-delegates voting. Assuming for sake of example, that voting in the primaries would tend to favor progressive candidates, if a progressive did not win the nomination on the first ballot, many more liberal delegates — the super-delegates — would enter the balloting on subsequent ballots, pushing the choice of the Democrat candidate for President toward the liberal side of the Party. In this way, the Democrats continued to try to limit the shift to the left that the increasing importance of primary elections was bringing to the nomination process. Again, the Republicans did not do anything like this, giving Trump a better chance of gaining the Republican nomination than progressives of winning the Democrat nomination.

The establishment (conservative in the Republican Party, liberal in the Democratic Party) has lost control for the moment of the presidential selection process in each party, giving populists and progressives a better chance of gaining the presidency in 2020 and beyond.

CHAPTER FIFTEEN

THE SURGE OF TRIBALISM

Tribalism, the racial, ethnic, gender, and sexual orientation identity of individuals, is at the heart of today's progressive Democrat politics. The basic proposition is that people of many identities have been exploited and discriminated against and should receive restitution for past and present mistreatment. So, Democrats, both progressive and liberal, support affirmative action in varying degrees to provide special treatment to aggrieved groups, and reparations to indemnify groups for past mistreatment. Republicans, both conservative and populist, join Democrats in supporting affirmative action to a limited degree, but are uncomfortable with the indemnities paid over and above affirmative action transfers.

In recent decades, the Democrats have made *identity politics* a key instrument of progressive agitation and the fulcrum of American political life. The concept is not new in America. Activists on the left devised it in the 1960s and 1970s to address the concerns of particular racial, religious, ethnic, sexual, social, and cultural groups.

The Democrats introduced identity politics to American national elections. Therefore, it is proper to analyze today's political situation in identity group terms, no matter how politically incorrect this may seem. Doing so illuminates the internal politics of the Democratic Party to a remarkable degree. It also illuminates a major political challenge facing the Republican Party.

Let us begin with the Republicans and identity politics.

During the 2016 primary campaign, I (Mills) asked Republican Senator Marco Rubio of Florida, then a candidate for the Republican nomination for president, "How will you respond to the Democrat use of identity politics in the presidential campaign?"

Senator Rubio replied quickly, "I don't believe in identity politics. Each person should vote for themselves without reference to a group."

"But," I responded, "to not believe in something is not a way to counter it, is it?"

The Senator did not answer me but turned his attention to another questioner.

Not only Senator Rubio, but Republicans generally, do not approve of identity politics. They retain a picture in their minds of each voter making up his or her own mind about who to vote for based on issues.

If Republicans practice identity politics a bit for themselves, they tend to do it incompetently. They aim at the identity group of white males who are only about 30 percent of the electorate, and an election cannot be won on their votes alone.

The essence of identity politics is to persuade each person to vote according to a group of which she or he is a member.

Identity politics make a choice among candidates easy for voters, just as party affiliation facilitates group bloc voting. If I always vote Democrat, I do not have to know a candidate's position on issues — I just have to vote for the Democrat. If I know that a candidate identifies with the gay community, then I do not have to care whether or not she or he is a Democrat or Republican, or know where the candidate stands on various issues. I just have to know that he or she is one of us — that is, one of the gay community or a strong supporter of it. I can even vote for a candidate who differs with me on important issues, for example economic issues, because I have confidence that on other issues that are important to the gay community as a whole, he or she will stand with our community. He or she is one of us.

Where a candidate stands on gay marriage is a signal to the gay community of identification or not. Where a candidate stands on abortion is a signal to feminists of identification or not.

Where a candidate stands on a border wall is a signal to Hispanics of identification or not. Many Hispanics seem to ask, "Why, if you want to put up a wall to exclude people like me, would I ever vote for you, regardless of your stands on issues like jobs or abortion or foreign policy or anything else?" So, to support the border wall is a signal that one does not support Hispanics across a range of political issues. To support gay marriage is a signal that one does support gays across a range of political issues.

There would appear to be something very deep in the foundation of identity politics that makes it a strong element of today's politics. We have seen this for more than 100 years in the politics of our big cities where large immigrant populations gathered, long before the coining of the term *identity politics*. In Boston, for example, Irish politicians took over the mayor's job from Anglo (Yankee) politicians and kept it until they surrendered it to politicians of a newer immigrant group, the Italians. In many large cities, European politicians have given up mayors' jobs to African-Americans who immigrated to the cities decades ago from the farms of the South.

Shared demographic characteristics are not the factor that binds identity groups together. One of us has an acquaintance who works eight hours a night and then sleeps briefly before going off to another full-time job during the day. Asked why he did this he explained, "I have to support eight children. I've never been married, but I have two children by each of four women. Three of the women are Hispanic, like I am. One is Anglo. Seven of my children look Hispanic like I do. One looks Anglo like his mother. And my other seven children all hate him because he looks Anglo." No issues drive this example of intra-family hatred but a sense of differing ethnic identity. This sort of group identification and dislike of those of other groups is a major contributor to identity politics. When Senator Rubio, himself Hispanic, says that he does not believe in identity politics, he seems to be expressing an ideal that would see each person as an individual independent of ethnic or racial identification. However, this opinion does not reflect the reality of the world. That is, he may not believe in identity politics, but it certainly exists and has deep and varied roots.

There is much more to politics than identity. There are many white men who are never-Trumpers, and in so being cannot be expressing gender and race identity politics — because they are of the same identity as Trump. It may seem surprising that so many white men are progressives, including some in the ranks of the leadership of the progressive movement, but it should not be. There is a body of white males who feel guilty, and which desires to make amends. It does so in part by supporting progressive efforts to seek retribution from all white males. Jared Sexton, in his book subtitled *Toxic Masculinity...*, recently wrote that "modern traditional American masculinity — more specifically white, cisgender masculinity ... includes tenets of societal privilege and white supremacy." (Jared Yates Sexton, *The Man They Wanted Me to Be: Toxic Masculinity and a Crisis of Our Own Making*, New York: Counterpoint, 2019.) The notion seems to be that the traditional concept of masculinity is toxic and that white men can escape it by embracing the tenets of progressivism. If within progressivism, white males are treated badly, the notion seems to be that they deserve it, and so will accept it. To populists, conservatives, and even many liberals, this seems a surprising demonstration of self-censure.

Identity politics plays a much broader role in American politics than influencing election behavior of voters. It also affects voters' outlooks. For example, identity politics appear to play a significant role in the extremely negative view that many voters hold of President Trump. On the basis of issues alone, it is hard to see why so many voters dislike him so intensely. His record does not seem to show actions or policies that are dramatically opposed to those promoted by his opponents. He has not embarked on wars; he has not thrown people out of work; he has not reduced the size of government, etc. He has certainly taken actions and promoted policies that Democrats have opposed, but not more so than other Republican presidents. Yet Trump is in a class by himself in terms of the abuse directed at him. It is possible to offer many explanations, including, for example, that he defeated Hillary Clinton unexpectedly and that this infuriated her supporters to a greater degree than previous defeats of Democratic candidates have infuriated the losers.

However, only a few years ago, George W. Bush defeated Al Gore unexpectedly, and much more controversially than Trump defeated Hillary Clinton. Yet Bush was not subjected to the level of vituperation that Trump confronted. Finally, Trump is not a traditional establishment Republican. He was a Democrat in New York City for much of his life and still thinks much like a New York Democrat. Traditional Republicans are acutely aware of this.

So from where does all the hatred of President Trump come? It is most likely attributable to identity politics. To many people, Trump is not one of their group — he is not gay; he is not Hispanic; he is not African-American; he is not Jewish; he is not a woman, and certainly not a feminist. What is he? He is a white male with traditional attitudes and behaviors who opposes much of the progressive agenda and liberal globalizing. Trump is hated much the way any white male anti-progressive or anti-globalist politician would be today.

Don't Tell Me What You Think, Tell Me What You Feel

Among the very important changes in our electorate are the increasing numbers of women voters. They will probably be a majority of voters in the 2020 election. Also important is the increasing energy of women voters about politics. Radical feminists are working diligently to turn women into an enormous identity bloc which can by itself sway presidential elections. Women as a voting bloc not only press for issues that concern women directly and largely exclusively, but also have opinions on issues of universal interest.

The radical feminist movement is very active today in American politics. With progressives — with whom it overlaps almost completely — it is one of the most powerful forces in American politics. Examples of the energy of feminist politics are readily at hand. One is the online invitation to a feminist cocktail party:

Tonight is the night! Be part of this fierce feminist cocktail party and celebrate the power of collective action. (Mass NOW, NOW via memberplanet.net, October 24, 2019.)

Note that the party is promised to be *fierce* and to celebrate the power of *collective action*. Fierce and action-oriented are good adjectives to describe feminist politics in America today. They are self-chosen adjectives.

In human affairs, how something is done is often as important as what is done. Relationships are as important as events. This seems to be especially the orientation of many women voters. The Republicans stress in their presidential campaign the accomplishments of the Trump Administration. However, many voters — particularly women — are less concerned with accomplishments than they are with the methods of the President. He is often viewed as unnecessarily crude and divisive, and as insulting to women. These perceptions, reinforced by years of anti-Trump media messaging, undercut positive responses to his policy positions and what he has accomplished.

In this way, the Democrats' continuing focus on the personality of the President seems to have borne fruit. Issues are lost in the flood of personality allusions. Voters who are too busy with their own concerns to pay much attention to political issues find it simple and comforting to respond to what many view as the undesirable aspect of the President's personality.

A Lost Opportunity

Many people seem to think that President Obama missed a once-in-a-lifetime chance to dramatically advance racial relations in America. Obama was the son of a black father and a white mother. He was raised for much of his youthful life by his white grandparents. When he became president, he could have chosen to declare himself neither black nor white but simply an American, and ask all Americans to put racial distinctions behind them. This was the opportunity he missed. Instead, he declared himself an African-American and engaged vigorously in the racial politics of America. The Democratic Party has followed his lead in that regard continuously since.

It is common for progressives, even among Democrats, to declare that each of their political opponents is a racist. There is no doubt that racism continues to exercise some influence in American society. However, many people, reflecting on how much American society has changed and how much their own attitudes have changed from those of their parents, resent being labeled racist for no other reason than their general political orientation. Nonetheless, African-Americans are a major voting bloc, an identity, in American politics. Democrats have their loyalty generally. In the 2020 election cycle, African-Americans mostly support liberal Democratic candidates. They seem uncomfortable with progressives' iconoclastic outlooks.

Identity politics carries over into the basic attitude of many people toward the American political situation. It affects far more than elections. It affects the ability of members of some groups to govern, and so impacts the performance of American democracy itself.

Identity politics and progressivism together have altered the American political landscape dramatically and seem to be in the process of changing it completely. It is the combination of the two that is so powerful. People for whom identity is a key factor in political orientation are now associated closely with other people for whom progressivism is the dominant factor in orientation. That is, people who think of themselves as an identity and care nothing for ideology and issues find themselves accepting progressivism by default.

Some people, of course, have multiple identities (an African-American who is a woman and is gay, for example, belongs to three identity groups). The Democrats try to make all three identities point Democrat.

However, reconciling three identities is difficult. In the contest among candidates for the 2020 presidential nomination of the Democratic Party, conflicts are arising in the Party between the many identities seeking the nomination.

Until 2008, Democratic presidents were all white males. In that year an African-American captured the Democratic nomination for president and then won the presidency. After two terms, Barack Obama surrendered the Oval Office. In 2016, a radical feminist captured the Democratic nomination and was expected to win the presidency and become the first woman president. Feminists were delighted. They thought it was their turn to win the White House. She lost the election. Feminists of all inclinations felt robbed. Many feel that the 2020 Democratic nomination belongs to them.

For the 2020 election, there is a contest among almost all of the various identity groups in the Democratic Party. Radical feminists feel that they deserve another shot at the presidency and there are multiple women candidates for the Democratic nomination. African-Americans would like another turn at the presidency so that there are several African-American candidates. Some African-American women candidates seek to gain support from both of two very large identity groups — women and African-Americans. Gays are seeking the presidency for themselves and have their first significant contestant, Pete Buttigieg. Jews have never held the presidency and there are several Jewish candidates for the 2020 nomination. Finally, white male heterosexuals (WMHs) are also seeking the nomination.

The contest for the Democratic nomination may be usefully examined in terms of identity politics. The initial leader in the contest, as measured by public opinion polls, was a WMH. Soon, attacks by radical feminist candidates weakened his position greatly and a radical feminist candidate moved into first place. The primaries were in large part contests of the identity groups to see which group could get the greater number of its members to the polls. The contestants were winnowed out until only a single candidate represented each identity group.

The contest among Democratic candidates began with a liberal who was also a WMH in the lead. Another WMH who was a strong progressive began to affect the political orientation of the candidates. Soon progressive views were being given voice by all candidates and several of the liberals withdrew from the contest or shifted their positions toward progressivism. The evolution of American politics is such that now the battle for the Democratic nomination for President is one in which progressivism dominates a contest among representatives of various identity groups. Liberalism is passively ceding the nomination. Progressivism for the moment seems to be triumphing.

On the Republican side, when there is a contest for the nomination for president, it is played out between conservatives and populists and several identity groups (women, WMHs, and African-Americans) although identity plays a much smaller role in the contest than it does in the Democratic Party.

Broadly, in American politics, if the demographic revolution continues to gain steam, the position of WMHs who are in the Democratic Party is likely to dwindle. They will be distrusted by the women, gay, etc. supporters of the demographic revolution.

A likely direction of evolution for identity politics in America is for WMHs to move into the Republican Party, only to be isolated there while other identity groups gather in the Democratic Party. Since that would threaten the Republicans with a permanently reduced voter base, Republicans are already seeking to counter the danger by widening the party tent.

A key element in this base-broadening is attracting a middle class of all races, genders, and sexual orientation. This would likely involve the movement of many people away from progressivism and the Democratic Party. It would be a significant response to the challenge of identity politics.

WMHs, whether they remain in the Democratic Party, or, like Donald Trump, become Republicans, seek the same tolerance for their views afforded to racial, religious, and ethnic minorities. They may succeed, but are swimming against the tide. Progressives will insist that WMHs cannot be trusted and should be barred from positions of authority in the progressive, Democratic and the Republican parties.

PART VI

POLITICS IN MOTION

We have a populist President who is trying to convert the Republican Party into a populist base. We have a progressive movement trying to subordinate WMHs, convert liberals, or drive liberals out of the Democratic Party. We have progressives slowly building private forces to fight those who contest unlimited entitlements, affirmative action, and restorative justice empire building. American politics are turbulent.

CHAPTER SIXTEEN

A PRESIDENT WITHOUT A PARTY

Trump has an Administration without a Party. He won the Presidency with virtually no populist support from Congressional Republican candidates. He has had to deal with an establishment Republican Party largely opposed to populist objectives. There is enough overlap between populist purposes and those of establishment Republicans that they can cooperate on some things. However, it is a difficult marriage that limits the populist agenda dramatically. That limitation in the initial years of Trump's presidency lead to the defeat of many Republicans in the 2018 elections. Those defeats handed the House of Representatives to the Democrats and created serious political problems including an agenda stalemate for the second two years of Trump's administration.

Populism has gained the presidency in the United States, but it is making only limited strides at the Congressional level — its success seems restricted to gaining the presidency because it lacks financial backers. Ironically, America seems to have a populist voting majority and a populist president but no populist political party — most Republicans are conservatives, not populists.

The partisan contest is within the establishment — between conservatives (Republicans) and liberals (Democrats). It may still be their game. The populists and progressives — the majority of the electorate — are excluded, except during elections when they can vote for what are mostly establishment candidates. Populists and progressives have benefited very little or not at all from the election and its results up until now, although, if a progressive wins the 2020 presidential election, he or she might dominate the Democratic Party.

There are very few, if any, populists currently in the House; none in the Senate. There are four well-publicized radical female progressives in the House (the "Squad": Alexandria Ocasio-Cortez of New York, Ilhan Omar of Minnesota, Ayanna Pressley of Massachusetts, and Rashida Tlaib of Michigan). Among the Democrats in the House and Senate who are liberals, many — especially the presidential candidates — are now turning to progressivism, giving hope to progressives for capturing the Democratic Party. The situation is fluid.

The media wing of the establishment confuses and misleads the population, preventing the electorate from appreciating the struggle between the establishment on one side, and progressives and populists on the other side, for controlling policy. Trump appealed to the masses against the "swamp". He was elected. Within a year, the establishment reined him in. If he were to govern in any degree, he had no alternative.

Populists have a voting majority and a president, but they do not have a political party and almost no legislators in federal government or state governments. It is of the upmost importance to note that Trump did not win the presidency in conjunction with, and as the candidate of, a populist political party. Instead, he won the nomination of a conservative political party (the Republicans) with deep roots in the establishment. He won the presidency at the head, not of a populist party, but of a conservative party. He won the presidency on a platform unsupported, except to a limited degree, by Republican Congresspersons. Early in his presidency, he tried to purge key Republican leaders and replace them with populists. He has made three major efforts to replace important Republican establishment figures with populists — two in Republican primaries in 2016 (Senator John McCain and Representative Paul Ryan) and then after he became President, a candidate for a post in Virginia. His favorites lost all the races in these primaries. As a result, Trump has been able to enact only a meager populist agenda. Trump and the Republican Party have been at great pains to obscure this basic point as they must cooperate to retain power. Nothing is gained if there is an open break between conservative Republicans and Trump populists.

Trump may be viewed as trying the best he can in this difficult situation to govern the country successfully and to win reelection. He wants to lead a movement but is only able to be titular head of the Republican Party. That is a key fact of today's American politics.

This is why Trump sometimes sounds like the leader of the Republican Party against the Democrats, and sometimes like the leader of an insurgency within the Republican Party. The two are not completely inconsistent with each other, so he tries to do both.

Trump's situation is very different from that of Emmanuel Macron, the President of France. They are both said to be outsiders who ran against establishment figures and won. Macron ran against the establishment at the head of a new political party. Macron won the presidency and control of the legislature (the National Assembly) at the same time. Macron has been able to do little with the power he gained, and he has called his failure to get reforms a "crisis of democracy."

Trump is in a much weaker position than Macron. In both countries, the establishment has very strong incentives to persuade politicians to be on its side. The establishment offers financial incentives of all sorts — salaries, fees, investment opportunities, and more — and so can attract political supporters. In the United Kingdom, a group of 21 members of Parliament deserted the Conservative Party on key votes in September 2019 to join with the establishment to delay or derail Brexit. In the United States, despite having won the presidency, populism has been able to shake very few politicians free of establishment ties. The result is that Trump has been able to get enacted only a small part of his agenda. In general, populists are less effective dealing with the establishment than progressives, who seem better at reconciling radical rhetoric with establishment ties. This is despite progressivism's denunciation of any accommodation with political enemies as treasonable. Progressivism is generally better at having its cake (radicalism) and eating it too (alliances with the baby boomer establishment).

The political consequence of this history is that, in the 2020 campaign, Trump has to do two things. He must win re-election and he has to bring along with him populist instead of conservative Republican office-holders — Congresspersons, Senators, governors, mayors, and state legislators. In other words, he needs to build a populist party in the legislatures of the country while trying to win reelection. As a result, Trump is traveling continually to different states to support Republican candidates who will back him in his populist agenda. Since most Republican candidates are neither supporting nor opposing Trump's re-election in a big way, he brings rallies to states in which there are local Republican candidates who will support him. At the rallies, he supports those candidates fully. He will not support Democrats who also support him — as he did not in 2019 Louisiana gubernatorial contest.

Thus, in the middle of the 2020 campaign, Trump is fighting a battle for control of the Republican Party simultaneously with a battle for re-election.

The control of the Democratic Party is being contested simultaneously. It is between progressives and liberals, and neither side has a champion of the wide-name recognition that Trump has.

Among Republicans, it is Trump for the populists against many potential leaders for the conservatives. Among Democrats, it is many potential leaders for the progressives against an array of potential leaders for the liberals. Simultaneously, many liberals are steadily switching to the progressive side.

Among Republicans, it is a simply understood contest; among Democrats, it is chaotic.

There is always a chance that Trump will disappear for one reason or another from the political scene. If this were to happen, it is possible that a charismatic upstart might articulate the populist cause and start transforming the Republican Party from within or forging an alternative party. Populists in America have been unable to generate leadership that is popular with voters until Trump — and Trump seized the leadership of the populist movement. He stepped into a void. This could happen again, but there is no indication of it yet.

CHAPTER SEVENTEEN

PROGRESSIVES TRY TO
DISPLACE LIBERALS

A n African-American minister told a friend of ours:

I speak from the pulpit. I know the people in my congregation respect the pulpit and I think they respect me. I tell them there is no free lunch. What the politicians are promising will be free will not be free. It still will have to be paid for in some way. No matter what the politicians say, you have to go earn it yourself. You have to work for it. There are no free lunches!

But I can't convince them. They listen to me, but they look away. Whether I speak to them in the church or as individuals, I can't convince them. It upsets me greatly.

This minister is telling his congregation that what the progressives are promising them is pie-in-the-sky. He is a liberal. Like other liberals, he is telling Democrats that they — the liberals — have learned some important things over many years of struggling for civil and labor rights. Liberals are saying that they have learned that gains do not come easily and that they must be earned. Liberals caution that patience is necessary to make progress and that the only secure gains are those won by effort, compromise, and follow-up work.

Liberalism has arisen out of the African-American churches via the civil rights movement, and has its origins in the masses. Liberalism is also kinder and gentler in its tactics than progressivism — it aims to persuade its opponents. Progressivism is combative.

Progressives currently hold no high-level government offices, although there are many supporters in high places among the Democrats. Progressivism is being strongly resisted by liberals who currently have the highest offices in the Democratic Party.

Progressives have unusual difficulty accepting continuing leadership. They respond to the most glib and imaginative in their ranks, but only briefly. The moment a leader ceases to keep up with the rapidly changing direction of radical thought, he or she is abandoned.

Progressives are rejecting the advice of the liberals. Without stable leadership, they are unable to make any concessions or accept any modifications or delays in the evolving radicalism of their agenda. They are carrying their message directly to the rank and file of the Democrats, and especially to the zealots who are sure to vote in the presidential primaries, but this may lead to a Pyrrhic victory. If they win the Democratic Party nomination, the Democratic Party may well lose the election to Trump. Progressives lack the liberals' popularity, and liberal Democratic Party funders harboring a grudge are apt to underfinance the 2020 presidential campaign.

Progressives give no weight to such risks. They counter-argue:

> You liberals have been too patient. We are not patient. Liberals are too willing to give in when there is resistance. Liberals are too willing to compromise when an opportunity is offered. Liberals don't go fast enough. Liberals haven't brought us to where we ought to be today.
>
> We progressives can accomplish much quicker. We don't want to be offered opportunity and then have to work to achieve results. If this is all liberals are offering, we are not interested. We want to get results now, not opportunities. The politicians are telling us that we deserve money directly from the government and that the government can get it by taxing very rich people. That sounds better to us than having to wait to get something. It sounds better than having to struggle to achieve results for ourselves.
>
> We progressives will use different methods than you liberals do. We will demand; we will not compromise; we will be rigid. We will use

political and legal weapons; we will weaponize government processes; we will criminalize what have been common political processes. We are on the popular side of a changing world and we will achieve what you could not achieve.

The arguments of progressives are gaining support steadily among Democratic voters, but only enough to split the Democratic Party, not to capture it.

Liberals Fight Back

Liberals are not pushovers politically. As progressives attacked liberal candidates for the Democratic nomination and injured one after another with the electorate, other liberals entered the contest. Among them were Michael Bloomberg and Deval Patrick.

Barack Obama, a liberal, lectured the progressives on the limitations he saw in their approach to politics.

This idea of purity and you're never compromised and you're always politically woke and all that stuff, you should get over that quickly.... The world is messy. There are ambiguities. People who do really good stuff have flaws.... One danger I see among young people particularly on college campuses ... I do get a sense sometimes now among certain young people, and this is accelerated by social media, there is this sense sometimes the way of me making change is to be as judgmental as possible about other people and that's enough.... If all you're doing is casting stones, you know, you're probably not going to get that far.

Thus spoke Barack Obama on October 29, 2019. This is the liberal speaking to the progressive. He is probably right. Unless progressives learn how to compromise better with liberals, the Democratic Party will lose its edge.

CHAPTER EIGHTEEN

WILL THERE BE FIGHTING IN THE STREETS?

Americal political culture is losing it civility. Threatening opponents, denouncing them, personal vilification, criminal charges, arrests, trials, jail sentences, public and private abuse, even some violence are now all elements of political controversy in America. It is possible to be sympathetic with the aspirations of America's aggrieved but still be disturbed by the mounting disharmony.

As progressives exercise their extreme attitudes and employ their radical means they prod rivals to dig in their heels and respond in kind.

For Trump and his supporters, the election of 2016 was the revolt of the common people against establishment excesses. For the left, it was a naked struggle for power between progressives and those who oppose their radical agenda. Hence, despite Hillary Clinton and Barack Obama's calls on the morning after the election for patience and acceptance of the result in adherence to the democratic process, there were partly violent demonstrations against Trump in New York City and the preparation of forthcoming riots in the inner city. The election was the end of a political campaign, and the beginning of an almost open conflict between the two political extremes in America.

As the depth of resistance to the Trump election became apparent, both Hillary Clinton and Barack Obama abandoned their moderate, Constitution-obeying rhetoric and joined the calls for resistance to and abuse of Trump.

Anti-fa — the militant wing of progressivism — began to attack conservative groups during the 2016 Presidential campaign. Generally, these attacks occurred on college campuses at speeches scheduled for conservative speakers, or at Republican rallies in the public spaces of cities and towns. If the cities and towns were governed by Democrats, law officers would sometimes be ordered by mayors to stand down and let the violence go on unchallenged. Often, the anti-fa wore face masks to conceal their identities. Generally, the violence was of limited extent — weapons were rarely used; guns were not employed; and people were rarely injured other than superficially. When anti-fa faced police restraint, they were not concerned. The civil rights movement and the anti-Vietnam War protestors had often been confronted by police. They were not embarrassed or unduly concerned by it. They conceived themselves as fighting for justice against the authorities.

Violence is deep in the DNA of progressives. Many 19th- and 20th-century socialists romanticized violence. Georges Sorel, an apostle of revolutionary syndicalism wrote in 1908, "There is something terrifying in ... violence.... But by undertaking this serious, formidable and sublime work socialists will raise themselves above our frivolous society and become worthy of showing a new path to the world." (Georges Sorel, *Reflections on Violence*, Dover Pub., 2012, p. 275.)

American populists, by contrast, generally support police and the authorities. They are disinclined to take to the streets. This passivity however may have limits if progressives go too far. As the Presidential campaign of 2020 takes form, anti-fa violence is growing more frequent and intense. By the summer of 2019 conservative and populist media, and the person-to-person communication of social media, began to report anti-fa violence with more concern — it had moved off the college campuses and from small cities and towns into the mainstream of American life.

Needless to say, the vast majority of Americans oppose anti-fa provocations, but this opposition may not be decisive. Violence may escalate, if progressives persuade themselves that is a winning gambit.

Plutarch tells us that "Pompey … used no other means against him [Caesar] than mere speeches and votes, for which Caesar cared nothing." Caesar turned to street violence and bribes and prevailed against Pompey in the Roman civil war of that time. Speeches and votes are the weapons of democracy, for which the progressive extreme cares nothing. For speeches and votes to be determinative of political outcomes, there must be a willingness on all sides to limit their actions to them. That willingness is disappearing in the United States.

PART VII

WHAT'S GOING ON

The threat of populism led by President Trump is allowing Democrats to raise more money for campaigns than ever before. This is an unintended consequence of progressive belligerence. The threat of progressivism is allowing the Republicans to reach new heights of fundraising, costing the Democratic Party and progressives with them the 2020 presidential election. Increasingly sophisticated computer technology of fundraising is allowing Republican fundraisers to milk their supporters like never before. The situation behind the 2020 Presidential campaign however is murky.

CHAPTER NINETEEN

I WON'T PAY FOR A LANDSLIDE

American elections involve parallel contests — one is for votes, the other is for campaign funds. Campaign funds turn into votes because campaign funds buy access to voters in a variety of ways — ads on TV or social media, travel, campaign workers, campaign literature — both legal and illegal. As Joseph Kennedy is supposed to have said, objecting to high costs when he was providing funds for votes to local sheriffs for his son Jack during the 1960 Democratic presidential primaries, "I'll pay for a victory but I won't pay for a landslide!"

Political fund-raising has reached new levels of sophistication. Now, there are innumerable campaigns, candidates, and causes to which a person can be asked to give. Computers compile lists of contributors and update them with each gift, and these lists are publicized in a variety of ways. Republicans keep lists of Democrats and vice versa. In consequence, Republican givers are almost never solicited by Democrats and Democratic givers are almost never solicited by Republicans. A new Democratic giver's name and contact information are shared with multiple Democratic entities and she/he is solicited by many. A new Republican giver's name and contact information are shared among multiple Republican entities and he/she is solicited by many. If a person attends an event for a candidate and never gives a donation to the candidate, he/she still gets continual solicitations — often two a day. Since there are voluminous records on anyone who ever gave to a candidate or an entity, if that person has ignored many solicitation since, emails will begin, "We haven't heard from you lately." If the prospective donor is on the Republican list, solicitations may begin, "President Trump wrote you; Vice President Pence wrote you; Majority Leader McConnell wrote you — why haven't you replied?" The emails get more and more personal.

"November 30, 2019. I emailed you. My sons, Don Jr. and Eric, both emailed you. Newt Gingrich emailed you. My campaign manager, Brad Parscale, emailed you. Trump Finance Team emailed you. Now I'm emailing you. Again."

"President Trump just reviewed the names of everyone who is entered to meet him in Chicago, and he noticed that William was MISSING from that list."

If the prospective donor is on the Democrat list, solicitations may begin, "Former President Obama wrote you; Speaker Pelosi wrote you; Senator Schumer wrote you — why haven't you replied?"

With a Presidential campaign which will consume two years and emails begging for money going out daily to a prospective donor, a generous donor can be bankrupted quickly. Finally, a prospective donor who ceases to give worries that he/she will be punished for it in some way. A prospective giver who finds himself/herself on both parties' lists will worry that he/she will be perceived as a traitor by both sides, and if he/she ever calls on a politician for help, will be looked up and given nothing. This all means that politicians can now respond to voters' requests, suggestions, or comments more accurately based on how much the voter has given to the politician or his party. Of course, politicians deny that this happens, and since there is no *quid pro quo* for a donation, the Supreme Court says it is perfectly legal.

The financial advantage in this campaign cycle seems to be with the Republicans. The Democrats may raise more money in total, but it is being consumed in great quantities in the primaries. The Republicans have no significant primary contests and so President Trump is raising large sums that will go almost entirely into the campaign against his Democratic opponent. To raise funds, the Trump campaign points out how much money the Democrats are raising in total, never mentioning that most of it is being spent on the primaries. The pitch is working — conservatives and some populists are pouring money into Republican campaign coffers, trying to match in total the giving that Democrats are receiving. It will be difficult for the Democratic candidate to raise enough money to counter Trump from a base of Democratic contributors who are already exhausted financially by appeals from primary candidates.

There are continual appeals for legislation to limit campaign funding. There seems little likelihood of that in the near future. A more effective, but indirect, approach might be to limit the length of our campaigns — if they were shorter, they might cost much less.

Looking beyond the presidential election to the government of the nation, it appears that in the United States, progressives are stronger politically than populists. This is because if progressives win the presidency, they will have a major political party, the Democratic Party, behind them. Progressive candidates for office at the national level are many and play a major role in the Democratic Party in both House and Senate. This is not true of the populists. If a populist, Trump or another, were to win the presidency again in 2020, he or she would have at most a few members of the House and perhaps a Senator or two behind him/her, because the Republican Party itself is still overwhelmingly conservative and not populist in orientation.

This will almost certainly continue to be the situation after the 2020 election. The contest in the Republican Party between populist and conservative remains heated. I (Mills) talked to the chair of the Republican Congressional Campaign Committee in mid-summer 2019. He is advising Republican candidates for 2020 neither to endorse Trump nor to abandon him, but to be neutral. So populists may again win the presidency as in 2016 but again fail to have an effective government.

From being an outsider spouting populist rhetoric, Trump has morphed into the leader of one of America's two establishment political parties. For the 2020 election, he has reverted to populist rhetoric but has the ability to deliver on his promises only marginally if he is elected — just as following the 2016 election.

Trump had been able in the 2016 presidential primaries and the national campaign to represent the populist insurgency. In the 2018 campaign he largely abandoned populism and ran primarily as an establishment Republican. The Republicans lost the House of Representatives.

In the future, it is almost certain that the presidential candidates of the two major parties will be a populist and a progressive and that may happen as soon as 2020. Trump has been a populist president. The Democrats are riven by a bitter struggle for control of the Party between progressives and liberals. The strongest argument that liberals make for control of the Party is that liberals are more likely to defeat Republicans at the national level. This implicitly concedes that the progressives are winning the control of the Party against the liberals. The tide of progressivism is so strong in the most active and committed of Democratic constituencies that a progressive is almost certain to win the nomination for presidency.

Populism is much weaker in the Republican Party than is progressivism in the Democratic Party. It is likely that the conservative, establishment wing of the Republican Party will again at some time capture the Republican nomination for president.

Put succinctly, progressives are in process of capturing the Democratic Party but populists are not near to capturing the Republican Party.

It is possible to view the American political scene today as one of reactions. Populism is a rising tide of reaction to the baby boomer establishment's mistreatment of the middle and working classes. Progressivism is a reaction to liberal gradualism.

It is possible that, in this presidential election cycle, we are seeing powerful backlashes by the overburdened and the impatient. If so, the strongest reaction will likely come from the progressive side. This is because populists are potentially able to command the presidency, but not either house of Congress. Conservative Republicans may win the House or Senate, but not populists. Progressives, in contrast, might gain the presidency and both houses of Congress in the 2020 election. If so, they will be able to initiate a legislative agenda. However, it is possible that that agenda will be unacceptable to most of the American population.

If a reaction to the progressive agenda comes, it may be brutal because progressives accept no limits of performance or merit on their objectives. So their apponents will feel driven to do the same. In this perspective, Trump is not the reaction, he is its predecessor.

CHAPTER TWENTY

WE KNOW THAT WOMAN!
CELEBRITIES IN POLITICS

I (Mills) had a friend who ran for Senator in a New England state. As the election drew near, his campaign ran several television ads featuring his wife. He had only a minor part in each ad, but his wife got considerable exposure. One morning, he and his wife were having breakfast at a local restaurant. My friend noticed that people at several nearby tables were watching him and his wife closely. This pleased him because he thought, "These people recognize me. They must know I'm running for the Senate. My message must be getting around." A few minutes later his wife got up from the table and went to the restroom leaving the candidate sitting alone. Immediately people from two tables got up and came over to the candidate. He looked up at them with a welcoming smile and got ready to exchange friendly hellos with them. But when they reached him, the people asked excitedly, "We know that woman you are with. We've seen her on TV. Who is she?"

This is today's America. The people didn't recognize the candidate for the Senate and weren't interested in him. But they recognized a face they had seen on TV and were very interested in her. She was a minor celebrity. He was not. And the celebrity got their notice.

My friend, who lost the Senate race, told me, "In today's America you need to be a celebrity to get elected to anything."

People tend to vote for candidates they know, and they think they know celebrities. People tend to vote for candidates they find interesting and entertaining and they find celebrities both interesting and entertaining. Celebrities have a leg up in electoral politics because voters are familiar with them. Celebrities have name recognition from voters. Political hopefuls who are not celebrities have to build name recognition with voters and it is a time-consuming and expensive process. America is a populous country with many voters, and it is almost impossible for a political candidate to meet most voters themselves. So name recognition has to be built by popular media — in movie houses, on TV, on the internet, and in social media.

For example, a Senator who is running for president may be well-known in his own state, but be unknown outside that state. If candidates are to be serious presidential contenders, they must become known nationally. A rough estimate used in current presidential campaigns is that building national name recognition for someone who doesn't have it costs somewhere over 100 million dollars in campaign funds. Even if that money is spent, the results could be bad — that is, the name recognition may come with a bad reputation rather than a good one, and so be disastrous.

In the 2020 presidential campaign for the Democratic nomination, Beto O'Rourke faced the challenge of building national name recognition. He had been a Texas congressman, hardly known outside his district. He ran for a seat in the Senate from Texas and in that campaign became well-known in Texas and among political junkies outside Texas. He lost the Senate election narrowly and decided to run for president. He needed badly to get known outside the state. Over some 10 months he spent a bit more than 70 million dollars campaigning to get his name known among Democratic primary voters. He succeeded to some degree in his campaign, but much of the name recognition he gained did not come with favorability. He was forced to withdraw from the campaign. All the money he had spent was wasted unless, of course, he could find some other way to benefit from the national name recognition he had acquired.

Even if Beto O'Rourke had won the Democratic primaries and become the Democratic nominee for president, he would still have faced the challenge of extending his name recognition beyond the

Democrats to independents and Republicans in the electorate. This is because a substantial portion of our electorate does not follow politics closely. Therefore, a politician aspiring for national office must find a way and bear the cost of building national name recognition.

However, those same Americans who make up much of our electorate and pay little attention to politics do follow entertainment and sports. It is an age of celebrities. Trump's success in 2016 was due in great part to his role as a media and TV celebrity. Millions knew him from his starring role on the TV series, *The Apprentice*. They didn't have a particularly favorable opinion of him, but they knew him and thought him entertaining — or more specifically, they thought him not boring.

A celebrity need not be liked. They need not even be viewed favorably. Celebrities need to be entertaining or interesting. Being a celebrity is a form of name recognition that is potentially very valuable in politics.

There are a few politicians who become celebrities. Former President Obama is one such. His wife, Michelle, is another. Since the polls show general name recognition for Michelle Obama and also show that her name recognition is favorable (she is the most popular woman in America), she is an ideal candidate for the presidency. Whether she wants to run, or could be persuaded to run, is a key question for the Democratic Party. In a presidential campaign against a Republican opponent, national name recognition would not guarantee her election, but it would allow her to start far ahead of other Democratic candidates. Oprah Winfrey is another celebrity whose national name recognition would make her an ideal candidate for president. Because these two women are so widely known, neither would have to make customary preparations for a run for the presidency. They could just announce their candidacy. The same was true of Donald Trump. When he decided to enter politics, he did not have to spend lots of time and money building name recognition. Celebrity status was enough to give him a long start in the campaigns.

Celebrity status has now become important in our national politics. The more than 20 initial candidates for the Democratic nomination for president for 2020 included no person with celebrity status. They were all being introduced to the nation's electorate. In the background stand several celebrities who, should they enter the race, might be expected to be immediate favorites because of their celebrity status — these include Michelle Obama and Oprah Winfrey.

At the state level, the Republicans, in particular, are seeking celebrities to run for state-wide offices such as Senator and Governor. For example, in Massachusetts, Tom Brady, quarterback of the New England Patriots football team was sought after to run for Senator. Knowledgeable people in both parties recognized that if he were to run, his general name recognition and positive reputation made him a going-away favorite to win the office.

Trump is the best evidence of the emergence of celebrity into a major factor in American politics. He might have won the Republican nomination for president and the office itself as a conservative, so strong is the appeal of celebrity status to voters despite political orientation and issues. But he decided to campaign on a populist platform. His celebrity status helped carry him into office.

Many voters, probably almost all, believe they know personally people who are celebrities. It is so common a phenomenon that it receives no notice now. However, it did in the early stages of television. People who watch other people on TV believe that they become acquainted with the people. They think they know them. They talk like they know them. I (Mills) have been fortunate over a long life to know many celebrities, particularly political celebrities. In day-to-day interactions with friends and acquaintances I continually hear things about a person I know. Sometimes the comments are critical; sometimes they are favorable. "He's so awful," or "She's so nice." I sometimes ask the person speaking, "Do you know them?" and "When was the last time you saw them?"

The answer is usually, "Oh, I don't know him. I would never want to meet HIM!" Or the answer is, "I haven't met her. Do you know her? Could you introduce me?"

The point is that the person who has such strong opinions about this person or that person usually doesn't know them at all — or at least doesn't know them personally, and has never met them. Yet the person speaking is certain that their opinion of the celebrity is correct. This happens usually because the person speaking has both seen the celebrity on TV and heard about him from other people.

It seems surprising that a person would make the choice as to whom to vote for on the basis of personality when they don't know the person or the person's opponents. Yet many Americans vote in exactly that way. They will tell you, "I vote for the person, not the party." If they knew the candidates, that might make sense. When they don't know them, it would seem more sensible to vote for a political party and its policy positions, but many Americans do not do that. They feel they know the candidates who are celebrities and they let that feeling good or bad dictate their vote.

This is not a reliable way to know about another person, celebrity or not. I sometimes ask, when I think the opinion being offered is especially wrong, "So you know this person only from the media — from seeing them on TV or reading about them in a newspaper?" If I challenge a person like this, they immediately take it as hostile and turn away. The question I have asked has its own answer — and none other. TV or newspapers are not a reliable guide to the character of another person, no matter how much a celebrity that person is.

Even celebrities have trouble gaining audiences when they enter politics. President Trump is proud of his series of well-attended rallies around the country. He attracts audiences of between 20,000 and 30,000 people, far larger than can be attracted by any other politician. But his audiences are dwarfed by the audiences attracted to rock concerts and football games. For example, a college football game between two major teams will attract over 100,000 people, and the audience would be greater if the stadium were larger. And on any fall Saturday, there are dozens of such well-attended games underway simultaneously. Much of the American electorate is simply more interested in football than in our politics.

Similarly, rock concerts are very often attended by huge audiences. Much of the American electorate is simply more interested in music than in our politics.

It is very hard for a politician to gain name recognition and to get the attention of American voters. Being a celebrity of one sort or another helps greatly. The strenuous efforts of populists and progressives to reach voters with their messages is hampered greatly by the inattention of voters and by their fascination with celebrities. America is not currently in economic crisis, so most of the electorate are not searching for radical political solutions. They are preoccupied with their personal lives. There is general dissatisfaction with the federal government, with national politicians, and with the struggle for livelihoods that so many people face. Nonetheless, this is far short of a revolutionary impulse. Despite the drift to extremes, serendipitous factors like celebrity could prove more decisive that identity politics.

PART VIII

OUR FUTURE

American politics has grown more personal and acrimonious. As this has happened, payback for personal insults and injuries has become more important in relationships among our political leaders. America's problems are going unresolved.

CHAPTER TWENTY ONE

THE POLITICS OF PAYBACK

Years ago, I (Mills) spoke with the top leadership of America's maritime industry. The industry had prospered with World War II. Afterwards, a series of labor–management disputes had slowly ruined it. There were many employers and many unions in the industry. Then, as in several other major industries, certain unions and their employers were allied against other unions and their employers — something almost never revealed in America's media — it apparently being too complicated for media audiences to comprehend. The opportunity to restore economic health to the industry by cooperation among the various blocs of unions and employers was evident. I went to them to try to see if this could be done. It couldn't and wasn't. One of the top union officials explained confidentially why what seemed so obvious a win–win for all involved could not be accomplished. "You have to understand," he told me, "that in this industry we spend all our time paying our antagonists back for what they did to us years ago." The blood feud took precedence over mutual gain. Settling vendettas was paramount.

The American federal government is now degenerating into something just like that. Democrats and Republicans have acted so badly toward each other that they both focus on paying each other back for transgressions. The most dramatic examples occur at the presidential level. Fifty years ago, the Democrats threatened impeachment and forced Richard Nixon from the presidency. In return, about 25 years ago, the Republicans sought to impeach President Clinton and failed.

On December 18, 2019, the Democratic Party dominated House of Representatives impeached President Trump. Needless to say, neither party admits that its efforts to impeach a president are motivated by a desire to get even. However, they are. The two parties retaliate tit-for-tat continually against each other in Congress.

The result is that the United States is now declining in the same way that our maritime industry did. It is a failure of leadership on an enormous scale.

Payback during the Trump years has injured the nation. The country has suffered more than the warring parties and is likely to continuing to do so until Democrats and Republicans put duty above their pettiness.

An epiphany is problematic because however the 2020 presidential election sorts itself out, one faction or another is likely to feel aggrieved. If a progressive becomes the Democratic presidential candidate and then loses, liberals will try to recapture the Democratic Party, making compromise and accommodation between the two parties more likely, but will also incense progressives. If a progressive wins the presidency, then, if they have a majority in both houses of Congress, unilaterally determined legislation, like Obama's Affordable Care Act, will certainly follow. This will further alienate conservatives and populists. If a progressive wins the presidency without control of both houses of Congress, then the progressive president will accept some compromise legislation in order to appear not to be a no-result president, but progressives will be encouraged to redouble their confrontational efforts. A progressive president in this scenario will fight a harder contest hoping to win re-election in 2024 and gain control of both houses of Congress.

If Trump wins the presidency in 2020, populists will try to make accommodation with Democrats on some legislation, even if Republicans control both houses of Congress, but if progressives lead the Democratic Party, accommodation of any political significance will be unattainable. If liberals lead the Democratic Party, some key pieces of legislation may be enacted on a bipartisan basis.

These are the several possible outcomes to the 2020 election. Progressives might dominate the White House and both houses of

Congress. Populists might do the same. The loser in either case is unlikely to be gracious.

One side or the other may win the White House, but lose one or both houses of Congress. Whatever the particulars, in the current hostile environment, prospects for bipartisan cooperation seem dim. Perpetual payback is likely to remain the order of the day.

This is discouraging. Much that needs to be done will not be done. The nation's physical infrastructure continues to deteriorate. Aspects of other countries such as bullet trains and modern airports continue to elude the United States. Billions upon billions are spent by the federal government. Tens of millions of Americans still seem to have inadequate access to healthcare. Poverty remains a problem for millions. Homelessness continues rising. Comprehensive immigration legislation is not forthcoming. Washington politicians seem much more focused on partisan squabbling and vendettas than on moving the nation forward.

As the political contest moves from being one between liberals and conservatives to one between populists and progressives, this situation is unlikely to improve. Instead, the Washington political scene may become more deadlocked and the nation more frustrated.

The politics of payback/frustration undercut the ability of a president to build an effective administration. The major players in any administration must be confirmed in their appointment by the Senate. During the Trump Administration, some of the confirmation hearings were so adversarial, and the confirmation processes generally so lengthy, that good appointees either withdrew their nominations after accepting, or simply refused to accept offers of government positions at all. No one could tell whether they would have a tolerable confirmation process.

The example of a friend of mine is instructive. He was offered a high-level post in the Trump Administration when it first took office. He did not personally know the President-elect. Nonetheless, he had been recommended to the people staffing the new Administration. My friend would have seemed ideal for the position. He had grown up in a Midwestern town to poor parents and made his way through college and into a job in a manufacturing company. He worked his way up to CEO of a moderate-sized manufacturer and then on to the top job in several other companies. He was the first American appointed to the board of directors of one of the largest German companies. He knew world business well.

However, once he had accepted the offer of the government job, a pre-confirmation investigation began. It consumed more than a year. He was interviewed by the FBI 10 times. Democrat-leaning newspapers began to ask about his private life. He had a wife and several children. They came under suspicion. Finally, with no confirmation hearings scheduled, he was asked by the FBI for yet another interview. "You had dinner in London 10 years ago with a group that included a foreign ambassador to the UK," he was told. "Who paid for that dinner?"

This was a final straw. Questions like this could go on forever. His personal reputation might be destroyed in the confirmation process in the way it was done to other appointees. He withdrew his name from nomination the next day. Other nominees had watched his experience and withdrawn.

It should be noted that the progressives' attack on white males in the Senate confirmation process was not purely partisan. It wasn't even, in a way, personal. It was a direct result of the ideology of American progressivism. As we pointed out in an earlier chapter, white males are condemned by progressives for many sins. One is that they reflect the tradition of manliness in our society rejected by progressives. The white males appointed to high office in the government, like my friend, generally reflect that tradition. As such, they are anathema to progressives. They are expected to repudiate traditional masculinity and condemn themselves for their past behavior, as do all white males who are progressive. It is their failure to toe the radical progressive line — to be politically correct in this important way — that is an important and usually unrecognized driver of their treatment by progressives.

As a result of how the progressives treated its appointees in the Senate confirmation process, the Administration was often staffed not by the best people, but by people who were available. By and large these people had their own agendas — a reason for accepting government positions despite the risk to reputation, fortune, and family. This was not the fault of the President, but of his political opponents. Nonetheless, it caused trouble for the President when less than the best appointees did less than the best jobs. The President was loyal to his appointees, in part because they had accepted appointments in miserable circumstances, but that only deepened the President's political difficulties when his appointees got into difficulty.

The people who refused government positions were not only Republicans. Some were independents. Some were even Democrats, because there are people who believe it their obligation to serve the nation when its leaders ask them to do so, regardless of the political party of the President. However, these people are no more willing to be pilloried in the media for accepting a government position than are Administration supporters.

Vendetta politics seems to ensure that when a Democrat again assumes the presidency, her or his appointees will be subject to the same abuse. The result will be the same — the best people will refuse government positions and the nation will be less well served than it could have been.

Will the electorate's increasing frustration break the deadlock soon? If history is any guide, the answer is no. Ordinarily, blood feud politics in America are resolved by outside events, especially wars that dramatically alter the political landscape.

This is not to say that each of the contending political forces do not have hopes of resolving the deadlock in its own favor. Each has a plan for a breakthrough victory at the polls that will give it a commanding majority in both houses of Congress and with control of the White House. This would seem possible. The Democrats won such control as recently as 2008 and the Republicans as recently as 2016. The stalemate was broken in both those years. Neither party used its advantage well enough to gain public support in the following elections. In 2010 the Democrats lost control of Congress and in 2018 the Republicans lost control of the House. Further, when each party had control, it used it for partisan purposes, not for the national interest. The Democrats passed the Affordable Care Act without consultation with or support from the Republicans and initiated a political battle over the Act that continues today. The Republicans in their turn focused on gaining control of the federal courts and ensured that, if and when the Democrats return to power, they will try to regain control of the courts.

In general, the politics of payback will ensure continuing bitter partisan controversy. Partisan stalemate will prevent the fulfillment of major national needs.

CHAPTER TWENTY TWO

WHAT A GOVERNMENT STALEMATE
IS GOING TO DO

Aprotracted political stalemate between Republicans and Democrats is possible in the United States. Control of the Congress and the presidency would pass back and forth between the two parties as it has been doing since World War II. When liberals dominated the Democratic Party and conservatives dominated the Republican Party, then compromises were possible, overt political campaigning was limited to only a small part of the year, and things got done. As political influence shifted to progressives in the Democratic Party and to populists in the Republican Party, compromise has become infrequent, overt political campaigning now never stops, and there is general stalemate with respect to problem-solving and legislation in our federal government.

We will briefly recount below the likely consequences of perpetual political stalemate. A thorough and deep analysis is possible but is more technical than is suitable here. Instead, we highlight the damage that we anticipate from the perspective of the welfare of American society. There are high social costs entailed by stalemate, which results in a failure to adopt by consensus government policies that are needed by our society.

In America today the partisan political contest — embittered by the rise of populism and progressivism — has virtually eliminated serious policy discussions across party lines. No progress is being made on developing potential solutions to key national problems.

Immigration is a key issue for both populists and progressives. It has both an economic and political impact. If America has open borders, then potentially tens of millions of immigrants would quickly arrive, drawn by welfare and other economic benefits. The traditional distinction between economic immigrants and refugees would cease to apply.

Populists fear that immigrants would take away jobs from American citizens and put downward pressure on middle class compensation, including the dilution of social security and Medicare. Progressive ideology calls for open movement of people around the world. Progressives argue that immigrants increase economic activity in America, but do not really care whether they increase or decrease the majority's quality of existence. They want to displace America's white male heterosexual *colonialist* culture. Progressives also expect to capture the votes of immigrants who become citizens or who vote in local elections without becoming citizens. Immigrants can tip the balance of power in American elections in the direction of Democrats indefinitely, both progressives and populists believe. In consequence, populists oppose open immigration and progressives support it. However, fearing voter resistance to increased immigration, progressives often pretend to qualify their quest for unrestricted immigration.

Most immigrants to the United States in recent years come from central America. They arrive after traveling through Mexico and often enter the United States illegally. Democrats and Republicans have been unwilling to enact a comprehensive immigration bill, so our southern border remains largely open to illegal immigration.

The openness of our southern border is now having another major impact. Through the border come large quantities of illegal drugs. Some are produced in China, exported to drug cartels headquartered in Mexico, smuggled across our southern border, and sold in the streets of America.

This trade in illegal drugs has spawned large drug cartels, most of which are now headquartered in Mexico. Mexico is a nation of over 100 million people that borders the United States. It is now a failing or even a failed state. Organizations that began as drug cartels have grown and diversified. They operate in the United States and in more than 40 other nations. They provide a substantial part of Mexico's economic activity. They also are involved in many sorts of crime and violence. The Mexican central government in the fall of 2019 withdrew its troops from a major city after losing a conflict with a major drug cartel. Media outlets in Mexico report that 80 percent of the nation is under the control of drug cartels or contested by them. The central government is said to control 20 percent of the nation.

In consequence, most Mexican citizens potentially could claim refugee status in America, or under a progressive regime enter America with no questions asked. A progressive American government, if true to its credo, will accept unlimited immigration from Mexico. A populist American government will try to limit this potential tidal wave from Mexico. The political calculation will be that, legally or illegally, these immigrants will add dramatically to the progressive vote and thereby solidify Democrat control of the federal government for an indefinite time forward.

In November 2019, nine Americans, mostly children, were massacred by a drug cartel in northern Mexico about 70 miles south of the Arizona border. The American President called for a war on the cartels. The President of Mexico immediately refused, saying that war had been tried before and failed. Former American military and border patrol personnel, furthermore, pointed out that if American police or military were to attack the drug cartels, the cartels could immediately retaliate against Americans in Mexico or the United States. In other words, the United States, like the Mexican government, is poorly positioned for armed combat with the cartels.

This situation greatly frustrates American populists. Populists have tried hard for several years to make illegal immigration and the openness of our southern border to entry for criminals of all sort and for intelligence agents of other countries a major political issue in the United States.

Populists note that China, Japan, and Singapore do not want any legal immigrants with clear pathways to citizenship and accept very few. Japan, for example, took only 27 refugees in 2018, but does have 1.4 million guest workers in mostly menial occupations. China has virtually no immigrants, legal or illegal, other than a small number of returning former Chinese nationals. The opposition of many countries to immigrants shunts immigrants in our direction. As climate change drives people from badly impacted areas in Africa, pressure for acceptance of immigrants in the rest of the world will increase. The European Union, without being explicit, now opposes open immigration, but is conflicted by obligations to former colonials and its official welcoming attitude toward refugees. Again, the EU's position shunts immigrants in the direction of the United States.

In a world which is being destabilized by population growth and climate change (whatever its causes), potential immigration to the United States is very large. Democrats, especially progressives, are likely to endorse immigration without limit and support the creation of a legal pathway to citizenship. The ulterior political purpose is to alter the balance of the electorate in favor of the Democrats.

Legislation is not required to have this happen, so control of the presidency and a strong position, if not control, in each house of Congress is all that is necessary politically for millions of immigrants to enter the country. This could be accomplished merely by failing to enforce the nation's current immigration laws.

For populists, limiting immigration is necessary in order to preserve job opportunities for current American citizens, slow the transformation of our national culture, and maintain a healthy political balance between Democrats and Republicans. In consequence, if populists can gain control of the presidency and Congress, restrictive immigration legislation is sure to follow. Democratic efforts to frustrate such legislation via sanctuary cities and states will be addressed by federal legislation outlawing sanctuaries. Because progressives view protection of immigrants, legal or illegal, as a moral imperative, a crisis is certain to result — one that will be fought out in the courts and likely in the streets.

Immigration is not the only important national issue affected by political stalemate. The performance of the nation's economy will deteriorate too. For example, even if President Trump reached an agreement with China about trade, it is possible that the Congress would fail to approve it. A result will be a continuing disruption of trade. Disruption will cause the loss of sales abroad and increase import costs.

Stalemate will also prevent Washington from a myriad of other reforms essential for increasing national competitiveness and fiscal prudence. It will impede domestic investment, impair employment, rekindle inflation, reduce sustainable growth, spur financial speculation, increase inequity, and might well trigger a mega-global financial crisis.

Very low interest rates and rapidly increasing indebtedness are building up serious financial imbalances. Low interest rates also stimulate financial speculation. Successful speculation — and there will be some — increases the extent of income and wealth inequality. The result is that another financial crisis is impending. A continuing political stalemate makes these unpleasant economic events more likely.

To the extent that climate change can be addressed by human action, political stalemate will preclude prudent action. Certainly, no unified national policy will be formulated. States will act on their own, and possibly valuable policies adopted in some states will be offset by opposite actions in others.

There will be no unified national antidrug policy. The lack of a comprehensive immigration policy will ensure that illegal drugs continue to flood into our country and deaths due to overdoses are likely to continue at a very high level.

American foreign policy will continue to seesaw back and forth between the desire of populists to reduce America's involvement abroad and that of progressives to advance a human rights agenda all over the globe. Foreign nations will be unable to perceive a consistent American foreign policy, making the risk of foreign wars higher as aggressive rivals take risks that American policy should have deterred. That is, war will be more likely than any sort of consistent American policy would have suggested.

Moderates, liberals, and conservatives each recognize the risks that continued government stalemates pose to the nation and its people.

They would accept negotiated compromises. Populists are also prepared to accept limited advances in their policy agenda to get some steps forward.

Progressives have a different *all or nothing, freedom or death* mindset. They believe that stalemate is preferable to compromise, in part because of their conviction that any forward movement on the populist agenda is bad for the country and for themselves politically.

CHAPTER TWENTY THREE

THE POLITICAL FUTURE OF POPULISM

Republicans continue to believe that the condition of the economy determines presidential election outcomes. If the economy is growing at a moderate rate; if inflation is low; and if the unemployment rate is low, then the incumbent should prevail in the election. Models of voting behavior which the Republicans rely upon use economic variables to drive their results. In 2019 economics-driven models show a Republican victory in 2020.

Liberals hold to much the same conviction — that economic conditions drive most voter behavior.

Progressives do not. Progressives are now convinced that other things drive how the majority of people vote. Among these things are identity (race and gender), cultural issues (gay marriage, abortion) and personalities (disgust with President Trump, for example).

Trump changing his residence to Florida greatly clarifies the political situation. The election is strongly regional. The Democrats will win the northeast and the west coast. The Republicans will take most of the south and some of the mountain states and the Midwest. The swing states are primarily Midwestern. Trump living in New York City confused all this to a degree. Now with Trump a Florida resident, he clearly represents the anti-coast (Northeast and Pacific) and pro-heartland voters.

The failure of the impeachment resolution to gain more than one Republican vote and Trump's relocation appears to have rattled the left. *The New York Times* ran a story recently saying that veterans of the

Iraq, Syria, and Afghanistan wars support Trump's desire to get out of those conflicts. This is remarkable in itself. And earlier this week, Barack Obama blasted the progressives — he is a liberal.

Trump speaks for populism in America at this point. However, he does not reach enough people to strengthen the movement greatly. Fox is the only major network that gives him fair coverage. The other networks generally, not always, spin his comments. His rallies are well attended, but in a country as large as the United States, simply do not reach enough people. For example, if he reaches 30,000 people at each rally and holds three rallies a week or 150 rallies a year, which would be a killing schedule, then he would speak to some 4.5 million people or about 2 percent of our electorate. If some of those rallies were televised this would increase the coverage, of course, maybe to 10 percent or so of our electorate. Other than that, the President must rely on what the media says of his positions and this is overwhelmingly negative.

So what will happen? Trump is not generally popular, at least as unreliable polls paint the picture. Years of calumny and vilification have damaged his reputation and his behavior has damaged his likeability. This result is another demonstration of the Nazi/Red rule of political propaganda — an oft-repeated lie will eventually be believed by most people.

Trump does not have long coattails for Republican candidates at this point. This does not matter much for the presidential election because in that contest everything turns on who the Democratic candidate is (as it did in 2016).

Trump no longer is the potential populist revolutionary that he was in the 2016 contest. He is now linked to the establishment via his connection to the Republican Party and its candidates. In both Mississippi and Kentucky, he appeared at rallies on behalf of the Republican candidates at the state level — and they are not populists though they embraced him personally.

The populist effort in America has so far been subdued. Populists won a presidential campaign and placed Donald Trump in the Oval Office. But, they gave him no Congressional support.

In effect, the establishment captured Trump — though he has already denied that. This is the perception of much of the populist electorate, who were called upon to vote for establishment Republicans simply because a populist president urged them to do so. They would not, and populists again in America have no alternative good political place to go. Trump was forced to ask populists who supported him to support the establishment Republican Party also. Populists do not find this appealing.

The populist movement is weak and possibly beaten for two reasons. First, the Republican Party has proven resistant to populism and to the policy initiatives of its leader, Donald Trump. Second, populists have failed to adequately articulate, refine, and effectively communicate their agenda to make it more broadly appealing. Populists have allowed their opponents to caricature them as reactionary anti-liberals and anti-progressives. If populists make their support for prudent, responsible, and tolerant social modernization clearer, then they could widen their tent. They do not oppose full employment, equal opportunity, moderate income-leveling, fair taxation, individual lifestyle choice, and optimal immigration. They only object to being the collateral damage of radical progressive and big government liberal agendas.

PART IX

THE IMMEDIATE FUTURE

A presidential election is pending in America. All political focus is on it. Populist common people and elitist progressives are contesting the election, and personalities are more and more at its center. This is surprising since Republicans and Democrats are moving further and further apart on national issues driven by populists and progressives. Where will these new forces in American politics take us?

CHAPTER TWENTY FOUR

AN ASTONISHING STORY

The polls tell an astonishing story about the electability of President Trump.

They told it before the 2016 election; they have told it all during his administration; and they tell it in advance of the 2020 election.

They say that if President Trump were to run unopposed, he would lose! Yes, if he were to have no opponent, he would lose the election. The polls tell us that a majority of Americans do not like Donald Trump and would not vote for him.

So, how is it that he may win re-election in 2020?

The answer is that when the Democrats name a candidate, the choice becomes a matter of the lesser of two evils rather than Trump's individual merit. An electoral majority of Americans preferred Trump to Hillary Clinton in 2016 and may well prefer Trump to whomever the Democrats nominate in 2020.

The evidence for this surmise from surveys taken in 2016 is very strong. Polls of voters leaving voting stations — so-called exit polls — showed that some 25 percent of the people who voted for Trump were not voting for him but against Hillary Clinton.

As some commentators have put it — Hillary Clinton is the only Democrat Trump could have beaten in 2016. She ran the only campaign that could have lost to him.

The same thing may happen in 2020. The key is whom the Democrats nominate as their candidate. Democrats persuaded by the polls that anyone can defeat Trump might once again choose a candidate that voters find even less appealing than him.

One would think that the Democrats would be careful not to let this happen. Yet most of the Democrats running for the nomination are positioning themselves to lose the election. For example, the Democrats have made identity politics work for them in many situations. However, in the current election cycle they are alienating many identity groups that might otherwise support them. They have been attacking people who hold religion dear, even though this may be a majority of the American population according to some surveys. They are alienating white male heterosexuals (WMHs) by labeling them racist, misogynists, exploiters, etc. WMHs are large group — about 30 percent of the electorate. Progressive periodicals like *The New York Times* count on *white guilt* to bring many WMH votes to the Democrats, but they may be pushing the point too hard, triggering a backlash.

Furthermore, since Democratic candidates for the nomination have pulled the Party to the progressive position, many potential voters who are not comfortable with elements of progressivism will have become unnerved at the prospect of an illiberal Democratic president. This is President Trump's strongest hope for re-election. Normally, in American politics, a nominee of either party who has moved to a radical position to get the nomination of his/her party will immediately upon nomination begin to move toward the center. Radical positions will be muted, and moderate ones expressed. This might happen with the Democrat nominee this time, but perhaps unconvincingly, if the candidate is a radical progressive. Moreover, time for feigning a move toward the center is running out. There are only a few months left before the Democrats select their candidate, and half of the time is in the summer. Most American voters pay little attention to politics during the summer — that is, before Labor Day signals the return of the year's normal work schedule. Moreover, the electorate is increasingly fragmented and hard to reach. So it is unclear that a progressivist candidate will have enough time to regain sufficient middle ground to attract a majority in the election.

As an incumbent who is well-known to the electorate, President Trump will not face this challenge. Trump's strongest chance for re-election is that the primary nomination process of the Democratic Party will choose as a candidate an abrasive progressive who an electoral majority of voters will reject in favor of Trump.

Trump may also have an advantage in the electoral college. This is why the Democrats complain so heatedly about the electoral college process which is established by the US Constitution. The electoral college is a procedure by which votes for president are rendered state by state. So it is possible to win the presidency without having an absolute majority of the votes cast nationally. In fact, Trump did so in 2016. Hillary Clinton won roughly four million more votes nationally than he did, receiving 48.2 percent of the vote, but Trump won the office, receiving 46.8 percent. Most other voters were libertarians (3.8 percent) who are close to the populists.

Some Democrats insist that since he lost the popular vote nationally, he should not be president (nor should Hillary Clinton because she did not receive an absolute Democratic majority either). Trump and his supporters simply point out that had the contest been scored differently — that is, by the majority of the popular vote nationwide, rather than state by state — then Trump would have campaigned differently and might well have won the popular vote nationally. It's as if American football were scored not by points (touchdowns, field goals, safeties, and extra points) but instead by how many yards each team gained when it had the ball. The game would then be played differently than it is. So if our elections were scored nationally rather than state by state, the campaigns would be managed very differently.

The Democrats in fact have an advantage from the electoral college that will be significant in the 2020 election. The Democrats have certain victories in many large states, so that their candidate need not campaign in those states. The Republicans have much less certainty in large states. For example, the Democrats are almost certain victors in California, New York, Illinois, and numerous other states on the east and west coasts. The Republicans are almost certain of victory in Texas, but no other large state. Florida, for example, is a swing state that could be won by either party. This means that the Democrats start with a long lead in the electoral college and need win far fewer contested states than the Republicans.

CPSIA information can be obtained
at www.ICGtesting.com
Printed in the USA
FSHW010055220520
70295FS

9 789811 218408